What Others are Saying About
DISCOVERING THE PURPOSE AND CALLING OF NATIONS

In view of current global events, "Discovering the Purpose and Calling of Nations" provides a timely warning, and is a clarion call to action to both leaders and citizens alike. It is based on thoroughly researched facts, and eternally relevant biblical truths; which makes it a must read for anyone with a desire to make a positive impact on their society, regardless of political affiliation.

The depth, scope and vision of the solutions provided, also make this book an excellent guide for future generations who will inevitably face the unique challenges of consolidating their national identity against the backdrop of an increasingly globalised world.

—Mrs Annette Dadzie-Banjoko
Business Analyst and Blogger

This is a classic book on the formation of nations. Dr. Sunday Adelaja, through intensive research, convincingly established the fact that nations are formed by God and are not a result of coincidence. It is research work for any person to study who is interested in changing a nation.

The book is built up slowing using different examples to simplify a rather complex topic. So, the reader needs to be patient and open minded because it is different from any book you ever read on how to change the course of a failing nation and make it great.

It combined historical information with evidences and biblical facts to convincingly make his case that every nation has the potential to be great and every nation has a specific calling.

The founding fathers of any nation, even African nations, all had this calling which is a mandate for their specific nation. The mandate is often communicated to the founding fathers of any nation by God and enshrined in each nation's founding documents, national anthems, pledges and national symbols. The great nations today are the ones that followed their calling to the letter. They are the ones that inculcated these callings in values for their people.

However, with time, lots of nations deviated from their calling. This deviation can be due to the fact that their descendants didn't understand these values and couldn't communicate them to the people to make them endure over time.

When you read his book it will give you hope that no matter how far away a nation has wandered away from their calling, they can still redeem themselves. However, this requires an understanding of how these nations deviated from their calling in the first place, so they can pursue an aggressive program of transformation in their society through changes in their value system. The main point is to identify these values and vigorously pursue them to be great.

This book shows that no nation is cursed. Every nation has the potential to be great through their callings. In the case of Nigeria, this book helps the people to identify the calling of the Nigerian nation and how to enshrine these values in the people.

This is a book that could change any failing nation. If you think Nigeria cannot be redeemed, then you need to read this book to understand the actions that must be taken to get this done and your role in it. It is much easier than you think, as Dr. Sunday Adelaja explained.

Dr. Aroms Aigbehi
Educator, Author, Life Coach and Founder of The Center
for Awareness and Critical Thinking (CACT)

In a world where most of us take for granted the blessings of nationalities and everything enshrined in our geographic and cultural idiosyncrasies, a world where there is a tendency and in fact has always been the case for one culture to dominate the others, where people are made to feel less because of their national identities, which is an integral part of who they are; there are often more questions than answers.

Dr. Sunday Adelaja comes up with this challenging masterpiece, who would have thought so deeply about the importance of founding values in a rapidly changing world? But this book opens the mind of the reader to the essentiality of the values enshrined in a nation's founding documents, symbols and history.

There is indeed a purpose for every nation, and no nation was born by mistake. One can see from DSA's artwork that the bane of many nations lies in their derailment from these founding values, and like the proverbial river that forgot its source, they begin to encounter avoidable challenges.

I have known DSA as a quintessential writer, but I'm truly blown away by his cognitive, scriptural and historical analysis in backing up his idea of nations having a divine purpose. I believe that, should anyone sit down to digest the content of this book, he will be fired up for more citizen responsibility and, if this book should be adopted into any nation's educational curriculum, then you can hope to see more national cohesion and acceptance.

As a Nigerian, I think with this book, every Nigerian can finally face the moment of truth, embrace our challenges, defeat them by going back to imbibe in ourselves values and principles upon which our nation was founded while standing proud of our national identity.

Dr. Bamisaye Victor
Medical Doctor, Author, Public Speaker, Poet, Preacher,
Mental Health Enthusiast, Social Activist

A good book is easy to read. It is often written in simple language, is well-laid out and is true to its theme. Moreover, it captures the reader's imagination from the word go, leaving him in anticipation of what's coming. The author of such a book does not shy away from detailed explanations where necessary, and yet, is careful not to overload his audience with too much information. This book does all of the above.

Dr. Sunday Adelaja has a penchant for explaining things that are hard to explain. His enquiring mind and insatiable thirst for knowledge often drives him to seek answers to questions many have been asking for years to no avail. And once he has found the answers he is looking for, he will often go on to discover what can be done to change the status quo and make things better. This wealth of knowledge and wisdom is then generously shared in his books. His books, therefore, offer a depth of information hard to find elsewhere and yet he is careful not to bore his audience with minutiae, striking a perfect balance between informing and maintaining focus on the overarching theme which, in most cases, is change.

This book is no different. In it, he offers unique insights into the origin of nations. He explains what makes some nations tick and others sick. He draws attention to the things most of us take for granted like national symbols, signalling their relevance to the calling of a nation. Drawing on a sound biblical perspective rooted in historical evidence, he helps to shed light on the factors that account for the rise and demise of nations without attempting to answer every single question about their existence. He shows the importance of going back to our roots if we want to understand the purpose of a nation.

As is typical of his books, DSA, as he is affectionately called, does not leave you with merely theoretical notions or historical accounts even though these are well covered, but he helps the reader to see how all of this applies to them. He highlights the role that politicians, community leaders, church leaders, the educational system and the media can play in helping to get nations back on track, but he does not leave out the ordinary citizen. He emphasises the relationship between the values we extol and disseminate in our families and their impact on the development of a national identity and encourages everyone to play their part in national transformation.

It is hard to finish reading this book without forming a

renewed interest in the history of your native country. I stopped reading after a couple of chapters to listen to and analyse my national anthem and was surprised what I found, and I am sure you will be too.

Dr Benedict Quartsin MD, MRCPsych,DipBA
Consultant Psychiatrist and life coach

WOW! If you ever need an answer to why nations are so different, this book is the key to unlock the answers for you. This is by far the best book I have ever read on nation greatness. Dr. Sunday Adelaja is an authority on national transformation because of his results. This is not just a book full of theories but rather a very practical book in understanding the reasons why nations are formed and how they have either deviated or stay on course of their purpose. I call this a practical manual for understanding and transforming nations.

The content is for everyone, both leaders and citizens. The book took a practical approach in examining key nations of the world and Nigeria. It looks at the reason for their formation by studying their history and understanding the values on which these nations were founded on. It later looked at where these nations are in respect to their national values. It is so glaring to see the reason behind decadence or progress in these nations.

Intriguing to me from the book is that the reasons for the formation of a nation are entrenched in the national values that are established by the founding fathers, and embodied in the national systems. It stated that the secret to the greatness of nations is hinged on its continued commitment to its foundational values.

The book doesn't just end at establishing the reasons for the founding of nations but also gave practical steps on how to restore any nation to its intended purpose.

In summary, the key to sustaining nation greatness is, national values must be integral to national development. These values must be engraved in the consciousness of citizens without which a country loses its identity and begins to die gradually from within.

As a passionate student of national transformation, this book is an intriguing masterpiece from my mentor Dr. Sunday Adelaja and it is highly recommended for every leader and citizens of any nation of the world. The principles in the book are universal.

Engr. Mathias Luka Agbu
Founder, Luka Agbu Memorial Foundation
www.agbufoundation.org

Wow! Dr. Sunday Adelaja has done it again as he always does with all his books, messages, articles, etc. One word to describe this book: Revolutionary!!!

Over the years, I had come to understand that every man has a calling to answer and a purpose given by God to fulfill on earth.

However, this book brought me a profound understanding that, not only does an individual have a calling, a whole nation does too. God has a purpose for every nation and not even one nation is accidental. God is as concerned about nations as He is about individuals.

As I read through the pages of this publication, the reality of God, His purposes and plans for nations became increasingly apparent to me. Hence, I'll like to refer to this book as the

"Nations Bible".

I believe this book is a must read for every citizen of every nation. The educational system of every nation needs to adopt this book for "Transformative Education", producing citizens whose goal is not just to be successful but equally responsible members of the society who conscientiously uphold and promote national values and ethics, wherever they find themselves. Without a doubt, this book would raise patriotic citizens who would stand for the advancement of their nations.

DSA previously established in his book "Nigeria and the Leadership Question" that the greatest problem with Nigeria is not with our leaders but the lack of value systems in the citizens. This book goes steps further to pinpoint our founding of national values and how they can be built into every citizen of the nation.

As a proud Nigerian, I can boldly declare that I see a generation of Nigerians who would become fully aware of the purpose and calling of God for our beloved country and would form in themselves values that are indicative of God's purpose and would lead to the progress of our nation.

Arise, o Compatriots, it's time to heed our call!

Dr. Anu Ojo
Author, Public Speaker, Life Coach, and
Founder Mind Revolution Initiatives

DISCOVERING
THE PURPOSE
AND
CALLING OF
NATIONS

National Greatness Starts From Here . . .

THE CORNERSTONE
PUBLISHING

SUNDAY ADELAJA

DISCOVERING THE PURPOSE AND CALLING OF NATIONS
National Greatness Starts From Here . . .
Copyright © 2018 by **Sunday Adelaja**

ISBN 978-1-944652-51-7

Published by
Cornerstone Publishing
A division of Cornerstone Creativity Group LLC
Phone: +1 (516)-547-4999
info@thecornerstonepublishers.com
www.thecornerstonepublishers.com

Cover designed by: Cornerstone Concept and Design

DEDICATION

This book is dedicated to the new generation of Christians who are not just satisfied with going to church to meet their needs but wish to go higher to influence nations. I pray that this book will help you to cause the purpose of God to come to pass in every nation of the world.

ACKNOWLEDGMENTS

I would like to acknowledge the editor of the book, Mr. Ola Aboderin, and I would also like to acknowledge the publisher Cornerstone Concept & Publishing and its president, Pastor Gbenga Showunmi for doing exceptional work.

CONTENTS

PART ONE
NATIONS AS MASTERPIECES OF DESTINY

CHAPTER ONE
- Sociological Perspectives
- Scriptural Perspective

CHAPTER TWO
- General Purposes of Nations
- Specific Purposes of Nations

CHAPTER THREE
- Retracing the roots
- Revisiting national symbols
- Returning to God and the Scripture
- Application of the Keys

PART THREE
ENGRAVING NATIONAL VALUES IN THE CONSCIOUSNESS OF A NATION

FOREWORD

Are nations born by accident? Do nations have a specific identity and destiny? Is God involved and at work behind those destinies? Is there a way to discover my nation's purpose? Could it be that most of our national crisis are due to loss of national original purposes and values?

Then how can we as a nation, return to our original purpose? And as an individual, what role should I play in this?

While most countries in the world and their specialists are focusing on economics or political matters to improve a nation's development and to find solutions to their respective crisis, Dr. Sunday Adelaja offers us a totally different perspective in his book, leading us to the origin and the roots of every nation, showing us that their future and success is embedded in their God-given peculiar identities and destinies.

Dr. Sunday provides us with a deep understanding of what is the essence and role of a nation.

One thing I particularly love is that he doesn't come with a minimalistic nor reducing approach, but he paints before our eyes the complete picture with spiritual, historical, cultural, societal, economic, and political points of view. I think that is what makes his work so unique: his analysis and presentation are not only intellectually relevant, but also powerfully, prophetically sound.

What will amaze you the most is that you will be enabled to identify your own nation's purpose, using the author's simple and logical method which is revealed through those pages.

Moreover, the book offers practical solutions after having demonstrated the deeper causes of our crisis. And those solutions will work and bring results at whatever level, either for the simplest citizen, or for the most sophisticated government on earth.

As a citizen, I found this book very useful and precious for personal knowledge as it changed my perspective and pushed me to a more responsible and proactive role.

As a Christian, I believe this book is a reference on the chosen topic because it contains and unveils in only one book, all the knowledge, the prophetic insight and also the practical solutions about God's actual purpose for nations.

As a French guy, I was excited, curious, then amazed and enlightened as I read the detailed, accurate and inspired analysis of the nation of France which is described in the book among other examples.

As a minister of the gospel with an international concern, I am grateful to the work Dr. Sunday has herewith released to us. I consider it as an indispensable tool and manual to work with.

I cannot but highly recommend everyone to read and absorb the knowledge contained in "DISCOVERING THE PURPOSE AND CALLING OF NATIONS"; and then to help putting it in every teacher's, every leader's, every minister's, every social activist's, and every government leader's hands.

A humble hearing and application of the simple truths contained in this book will change nations.

Pierre-Emmanuel JEAN
Pastor, author, international speaker, Gospel artist, founder
and leader of Mission Gospel Centre (France)

PREFACE

This book, Discovering the Purpose and Calling of Nations, is one of the most fulfilling works I have done. Lately, I have been writing a lot concerning my home country of Nigeria and the African continent in general. But I have always wanted to write a book for the nations of the world. I somehow feel in my heart that it is not fair to other nations, for me to just focus all my attention to either eastern Europe or Africa. Moreover, I strongly feel that I have what to tell the nations of the world. Even though there is a long list of subjects I will like to raise for discussion before the nations, yet I feel this book is starting at the right place. The second title for "Discovering the Purpose and Calling of Nations" is "National greatness begins from here..."

Yes, this book addresses where it all begins. Any kind of greatness, especially national greatness, begins from discovering purpose. I am especially satisfied that I am starting my discourse with the nations of the earth with this particular book. What are the things you must look forward to in this book:

First, you will discover that nations are masterpieces of destiny. That is to say, nations are not by accident, including your nation. Sometimes, when we see what is happening in our nations, we are tempted to think that something is wrong. Some might even think their nations are a mistake. This book will tell you otherwise. There is a purpose for every nation. A pre-ordained purpose by God. But more importantly than this, Discovering the Purpose and Calling of Nations, will help you to unlock God's masterplan for your country.

In this book, I am providing the blueprint to help every person to find out what God's intentions for his or her country are. The formulas are well spelt out, such that no one will miss the point.

Another very important junction in this book is the fact that we have endeavored to demonstrate by examples for all our readers, the process of discovering purpose and callings of nations. We have chosen five significant countries of our world as illustrations so that when our readers see the illustrated process to which we outlined the calling and purpose of each of these nations, it will now be much easier for the reader to go through the same process in regards to his or her nation. The five countries we have chosen to use are:

1. The United States of America (the nation in a rendez-vous with destiny),
2. Nigeria (the blessed giant with the thinking problem),
3. France (the spectacular thinker with a peculiar stinker),
4. Germany (the pacesetter through peacemaking),
5. The United Kingdom (the preserver of ancient values).

In the third part of this book, I also try to touch on the process it will take to engrave each nation's national values in the consciousness of the people. Unfortunately, today many citizens have not endeavored to discover their nation's national values, talk less of engraving them in their consciousness. The tragic result is, for example, the problem of obesity is no longer an American problem, but fast becoming a global problem, as a result of all countries copying the American fast food lifestyle. Homicide has long stopped to be just a New York City problem, it is now a global problem, because nations of the world now depend on Hollywood to get their values. So in a situation when nations fail to define their national values, they become victims of strange cultures that are imposed upon them through television, movies, etc. This book will help every nation preserve their uniqueness, thereby fulfilling their national purpose and calling.

There is a lot to write and say about this book, the only writing to do from now on is to do your best to painstakingly to go through every page and every word in this book, so that you will join the company of nation builders.

For the love of God, Church and Nation,
Dr. Sunday Adelaja

INTRODUCTION

It was Marcus Garvey, the Jamaican political leader and orator, who once said, "There is no force like success, and that is why the individual makes all effort to surround himself throughout life with the evidence of it; as of the individual, so should it be of the nation."

I have no doubt in my mind that the pursuit of greatness is at the core of the aspirations of the nations of the world. Regardless of internal conflicts and instabilities, every true nation collectively seeks to surpass the other and, indeed, yearns to be the grand spectacle of success, progress and superiority in every state of its affairs.

However, as I observe the state of most nations of the world, especially from a scriptural point of view, I discover two alarming trends. On the one hand is widespread misconception about the true nature of greatness – what really makes a nation great? Is it just its political, economic and military might and supremacy? This confusion is common especially with reference to most so-called developed nations of the world. Can a nation, for example, be described as being truly great when despite massive economic, technological and scientific advancements, the citizens continue to wallow in the cesspool of decadence, perversions, mind-boggling crimes, as well as rampant cases of discontent, depression, disillusionment, drug dependence, dreadful diseases and disturbing deaths?

On the other hand is pervasive ignorance about what it really takes to escape the quagmire of socio-economic stagnation, political crises and technological backwardness, and become a vibrant, self-reliant entity. This is associated with many third-world, struggling nations. Why, for example, do many of these nations remain perpetual beggars and puppets of the developed nations in order to survive? Why is it that years of receiving aids and other forms of support have not improved the lots of these countries by any standard?

It was my desire to demystify these concerns and provide clear, credible and practical answers to the numerous questions surrounding national greatness that prompted me to write this book. The goals I proposed to achieve through this publication can be seen from the three distinct parts into which it is divided. My first goal is to establish the fact that upon every nation is a unique calling of God, within which is embedded the seed of true greatness that has proved elusive to many. Secondly, I wish to show citizens of every nation the secrets of ascertaining this calling and unlocking its boundless possibilities. Lastly, I wish to present to every nation some ideas on steps that will facilitate maximum enjoyment of the manifold blessings in following God's calling for them.

I believe that the essence of revelation is liberation. With the knowledge of the truth comes absolute freedom from all limitations (John 8:32). The reason almost every nation of the world is bound by fetters – whether spiritual, moral, economic or environmental - is either ignorance or loss of the divine calling. Consequently, I have come to realize that when nations are roused to the knowledge of their callings and the corresponding prospects and possibilities; when institutions are established and strengthened to work towards the implementation of these callings; when citizens are systemically enlightened and collectively mobilized to move in the direction of their preordained destinies - then they become automatically armed with a powerful sense of direction, which will eventually lead them to all-inclusive greatness and fulfillment.

Christian families, leaders, ministers, missionaries and intercessors, in particular, need to understand God's calling for their nations, in order to be effective in their prayers and outreaches. We have been raised as watchmen and expediters of God's eternal purposes in our nations. But how do we do this without enabling knowledge? The reason the children of Issachar were effective in mobilizing and leading their brethren was because they had exclusive knowledge of what needed to be done at the right time to safeguard their nation! (1 Chronicles 12:32).

More importantly, Christ enjoined us to pray that God's will be done on earth as it is in heaven, and this must be applied to our nations. Beyond that, however, we have been empowered and assured that whatsoever we bind or loose on earth shall be sanctioned in heaven. We have a duty therefore, perhaps more binding than what is expected of our fellow citizens, to find out what is the particular will (calling, purpose, program) of God for our nation and labor prayerfully and patriotically for its actualization.

PART ONE

NATIONS AS MASTERPIECES OF DESTINY

CHAPTER ONE

NATIONS ARE NOT BY ACCIDENT

This is one fact that I wish to establish from the very outset of my exploration of the secrets of national greatness. The reason is simple. Only with this foundational insight can we understand the true essence, calling, significance and destiny of every nation.

I am aware that many events on earth are often considered accidental or coincidental because they are believed to have happened by chance or unexpectedly. Whether such claims of coincidence are true or not is dependent on an independent analysis of the circumstances surrounding each of such occurrences. However, from my studies on the subject of the evolution of nations, I would say that the claim of accident or coincidence for nations is practically non-existent.

Let me begin with the meaning of the word itself. While controversies abound (as they often do among intellectuals) as to the exact definition of "nation", most scholars agree that a nation is "a large body of people united by common descent, history, culture, or language, inhabiting a particular state or territory."

The Etymological Dictionary, which deals with the origin of

words, says "nation" is directly from the Latin word nationem which can mean "birthplace," "race of people", "tribe", or even more literally "that which has been born". Essentially then, a nation can be said to consist of people or groups of people who share similar territorial, historical, cultural, linguistic, ethnic and symbolic identity.

Now, recent statistics show that there are about 196 independent nations in the world today. The question is, what accounts for the formation of these nations? How do "large bodies" of different individuals, races, tribes and ethnic groups, who sometimes even speak different languages, come together to form a nation and pursue common interests? Or I might even go further by asking, how were the distinguishing boundaries, cultures and value systems of these nations determined and established? Was it all a result of random, accidental happenings or was there a binding factor or, better still, a DRIVING FORCE behind these formations?

SOCIOLOGICAL PERSPECTIVES

Even from a purely human perspective, that is, from a historical, sociological or even political viewpoint, scholars agree that nations never emerge spontaneously. Analysts unanimously believe that their formation is often predicated on a series of factors, events, yearnings and aspirations. Functionalist interpreters of the concept of nationalism, for example, believe that nations are founded upon "individuals' concerns over distribution of resources acquired through individual and collective action."1 This concern is then resolved by the formation of a clan group that defines who is accepted within the group and defines the boundaries within which the resources will be distributed.

In the article, "The Formation of Nations", posted on the *Nationalism Studies* blog on March 19, 2010, the author stated, "Even though nations were processes which drew boundaries, they were very much formed by people who were relatively free to travel **without such bounded restrictions.**"2

Looking at this, I am compelled to ask, once again: why would people, who are free to travel about, willingly choose to bound themselves together and forge an identity and, indeed, a destiny for themselves? There must be an overriding goal, far from being accidental!

In his highly influential speech, *What is a Nation?* (presented in 1882), Ernest Renan explains this notion even more clearly when he said, "The modern nation is therefore a historical result brought about by a series of convergent facts. Sometimes unity has been effected by a dynasty, as was the case in France; sometimes it has been brought about by the direct will of provinces, as was the case with Holland, Switzerland, and Belgium; sometimes it has been the work of a general consciousness, belatedly victorious over the caprices of feudalism, as was the case in Italy and Germany. These formations always **had a profound raison d'etre** (reason for existing or happening)."

Indeed, I personally believe that there is a raison d'etre behind the materialization of every nation. The fact that every nation on earth has a root, a unique name, an identity and a birth date - which is usually the date of its independence (the date the citizens began to govern themselves as a nation) or the date it unveils its constitution - is enough proof that there is more to the formation of a nation than mere accidental exigencies.

Peter Ravn Rasmussen, in his July 2001 article, *"Nations" or "States"?: An Attempt at Definition*, affirms this, by saying, "Tribalism aside, the bonds that bind a group of people into a nation are more complex than mere blood relationships (real or imagined). This relationship really only holds true at the lowest levels of society (and even then, local hierarchies related by blood have become rare in the modern world). As civilized society grows ever more complex, it is often the case that nationality is a function of more complex factors - a shared heritage or blood relationship being only one of them."3

Even in the case of countries like Singapore, whose independence a few assume to have been solely and prematurely triggered by an external force (Malaysia), there are facts to prove that their creations were never accidental. Writing about Singapore, for example, Mr. Palaniyapan of Singapore Matters blog, said emphatically:

"Looking deeply, one would find that though it was Malaysia which broached the topic of secession first, the move was to a large extent precipitated by Singapore's actions. The conclusion that Singapore is an accidental nation is an erroneous and dangerous conclusion to draw...Far from being passive agents, we were active agents in the lead up to the independence. By accepting our agency in our independence, we are more likely to give these important moments in our history their due place in our national narrative."4

SCRIPTURAL PERSPECTIVE

Now that I have given myriads of proofs from scholars about the purposeful creation of nations, let me now make references to the Scripture. The Bible, which is the most credible authority on the creation of the world, offers greater and much deeper insights on this subject. Genesis alone, which is fittingly referred to as the "book of beginnings" has several references to God's direct involvement in the creation of nations – a pointer to the fact that nations are not accidental formations.

Let me put it more directly, the fact that God was, from the beginning, involved in the creation, composition and distribution of nations is the most convincing proof that no nation could be described as accidental, since God is never involved in accidents.

34

"Known to God from eternity are all His works" (Acts 15:18).

So, what specifically does the Bible say about the formation of nations? Let me show you:

1. God conceived the notion of nations and nationalities from the beginning.

It was the intention of God from the beginning of creation that mankind should increase, multiply and take possession of the ends of the earth (Genesis 1:28). God emphasized the scope and seriousness of this objective when He frustrated the building of the Tower of Babel. What happened then was that the inhabitants of the earth had converged and conspired to confine themselves to a particular location, contrary to the divine plan for them to disperse. They had said, **"Come, let us build ourselves a city, and a tower whose top is in the heavens; let us make a name for ourselves, lest we be scattered abroad over the face of the whole earth"** (Genesis 11:4).

God therefore had to redirect them to his original purpose by breaking them up into different linguistic units, which made it possible for individuals sharing a particular language to begin to align and associate with one another – a core characteristic and precursor of what we now know to be nationalism. **"Therefore its name is called Babel, because there the Lord confused the language of all the earth; and from there the Lord scattered them abroad over the face of all the earth"** (verse 9).

2. God orchestrated the foundation, formation and dispersion of nations.

After the destruction of the old, sinful world, through the instrumentality of a flood, the Bible says that God, whose eternal purposes and plan can never be changed by the changeability of man, still went ahead to lay the foundation for the formation, diversification and dispersion of the nations of the world through the three sons of Noah - Shem, Ham and Japheth. Genesis 10:32 says, **"These were the families of the sons of Noah, according to their generations, in their nations; and from these the nations were divided on the earth after the flood."**

It may interest you to know that researchers have found out that all nations of the earth derive their distinctive characteristics from the particular son of Noah to whom their ancestry can be traced. In the past century, scholars like George Rawlinson, famous for his Origin of Nations (1878); Archibald Sayce, in such books as Races of the Old Testament (1891; 1925); Alonzo T. Johnes in The Peopling of the Earth (1887) and The Empires of the Bible (vol. 1) (1904), took special interest in this chapter of the Bible (Genesis 10) in their quest to trace the "family tree" of the nations of the earth. Their findings were not only enlightening but equally astonishing.

Following in the footsteps of the above scholars, some scholars in this century also, including Dr. Herman L. Hoeh, Arthur C. Custance, Dr. D. J. Wiseman, Dr. John Pilkey, Bill Cooper, J. Simon and Ross Marshall, have all demonstrated that the biblical account of the origin of the nations of the earth is compellingly credible – a proof that nations exist, not by accident but according to the eternal purpose of God.

3. God still orchestrates the emergence and dominance of nations.

In keeping to His purpose and will, God is still in the business of triggering the birth of nations, whether by revolution, secession, independence or any other means by which nations assume self-determination and self-rule. The Bible records that God specifically told Abraham in Genesis 17:6: **"...I will make nations of you, and kings shall come from you."** To Rebekah's enquiry on why the set of twins in her womb constantly struggled with each other, God told her in Genesis 25:23. **"Two nations are in your womb, two peoples shall be separated from your body; One people shall be stronger than the other, And the older shall serve the younger.**

Sometimes people mistakenly think that empires, kingdoms and nations emerge and become dominant due to some random circumstances or chains of events. But the Bible says that God's hand is behind these circumstances. Job 22:23 says, **"He makes nations great, and destroys them; He enlarges nations, and guides them."** Even concerning the emergence of world "superpowers", as well as the duration of their reign, the Scripture tells us that God has all the answers. Daniel 4:17 says, **"…the Most High rules in the kingdom of men, gives it to whomever He will, and sets over it the lowest of men."**

4. God has foreknowledge of the locations and character traits of nations.

God is involved in forecasting the unique behavioral patterns, locations, boundaries and natural resources of the nations of the world. As Acts 17:26 reveals: **"And He has made from one blood every nation of men to dwell on all the face of the earth, and has determined their preappointed times and the boundaries of their dwellings"**

Specifically, for the nation of Israel, Ezekiel 5:5 says, **"Thus says the Lord God: 'This is Jerusalem; I have set her in the midst of the nations and the countries all around her."** God purposely positioned the nation of Israel to be where it currently occupies today, as well as the nations surrounding it, and by extension, all the nations of the earth. Whether humans know it or not, God's program is playing out in the daily interactions and events occurring between and among these nations.

On the peculiar behavioral patterns of individual nations, there is ample evidence from the Bible that none of them is accidental. Of the idiosyncrasy of the Arabic nations, for example, God had predicted through Ishmael, from whom they emerged: **"He shall be a wild man; His hand shall be against every man, And every man's hand against him. And he shall dwell in the presence of all his brethren"** (Genesis 16:12).

5. God actively monitors and oversees events in all nations.

There are people who think God is only interested in what goes on in the nation of Israel, but this is far from being true. In reality, God is actively interested and involved in the affairs of every nation that He has caused to be created. Psalm 66:7 puts it in clearer terms, **"He rules by His power forever; His eyes observe the nations..."**

Regarding the emergence of national governments and leaders, the Scripture says God is fully interested and involved. Romans 13:1 emphatically exhorts: **"Let every soul be subject to the governing authorities. For there is no authority except from God, and the authorities that exist are appointed by God."**

6. God could decide the subjugation/extinction of a nation.

Does the subjugation of a nation by another catch God unawares? Can we say that colonialism, however unpleasant it may sound to the colonized, was an accident of history? I don't think so, as the Bible answers to the contrary. Jeremiah 28:14 says, **"For thus says the Lord of hosts, the God of Israel: "I have put a yoke of iron on the neck of all these nations, that they may serve Nebuchadnezzar king of Babylon; and they shall serve him..."**

Of course, to Nebuchadnezzar and all the nations under his temporary dominion, it might seem that military might or superior battle strategy gave him overwhelming control. But, as I have shown you, God said it was all according to His preordained will. He was involved in the entire process, and so it is today in our current world.

How about nations that once existed but have now become extinct? Were their disappearances accidental? Not at all. God says, for instance, in Zephaniah 3:6 **"I have cut off nations, their fortresses are devastated; I have made their streets desolate, With none passing by. Their cities are destroyed; there is no one, no inhabitant."**

7. Nations have specific angels/demons (territorial spirits) attached to them.

Let me tell you that nations are so important in the overall program of God that there are specific angels assigned to them to see to the fulfillment of God's purpose for them. They do this by communicating the minds of God to the nation through their spiritual leaders, as well as spiritually influencing the people, especially leaders at all levels, to align with the program of God and lead the people into doing same.

On the other hand, however, Satan, too, has his demons attached to the various nations to thwart the will of God for them. They do these by enticing people away from God, triggering crises and calamities, fighting against the Church of God and preventing answers to prayers made for the nation. Many theologians believe that the "sons of God" that are said to present themselves before Him in Job 1:6 are the guardian angels of the existing nations as at then. But more specifically, in Daniel 10, glaring references were made to the Prince (angel) of the nation of Persia (verses 12-13), the Prince of Greece (verse 20) and the Prince of the nation of Israel (verse 21).

I could go on and on, but the bottom-line should have been established by now - nothing is accidental about the origin, identity, location, status or destiny of any nation. Behind all that we see in the physical is the unseen hand of the Almighty God, starting, shaping and stirring events towards the fulfillment of His ultimate purpose and program for every nation. **"For the kingdom is the Lord's, And He rules over the nations"** (Psalm 22:28).

CHAPTER TWO

GOD PREORDAINS NATIONAL PURPOSE

N ow that I have shown you from different perspectives that nations do not emerge by accident, but by God's design, you may want to ask me: *"to what intent?"*

Let me begin to answer this question by reaffirming that God indeed is not a God of impulse but a God of purpose, order and knowledge. Nothing happens anywhere or at any time without His knowledge; and if He allows anything to happen, including the birth of a nation, it is for a reason.

The Bible declares that **"All things were made by Him; and without Him was not any thing made that was made"** (John 1:3). I believe that these "all things" include nations and cultures of the world. Of course, I know that there are aspects of certain cultures that appear barbaric, repugnant and indeed ungodly; but you must also remember that the corruption that ensued from the fall of man also affected his thinking and behavior – which makes it easy for him to pervert what God intended for good.

Ecclesiastes 7:29 says, **"Truly, this only I have found: That God made man upright, But they have sought out many schemes."** So, the fact that many abhorrent practices are carried out in the name of cultures, customs and traditions does not overrule the truth that God is involved in the origination of these cultures, or that he has no specific reasons in mind.

Even among human beings (which incidentally are created in the likeness of God), nothing is instituted, invented or produced without a purpose. Every single man-made object or entity, however small or large, was conceptualized, designed and manufactured with a goal in mind. How much more the things, beings and nations created by God!

One other thing you must note is that while nations and cultures may seem many and varied, they are not as many as the stars of heaven, the number of which God fully knows; in fact, **"He calleth them all by their names"** (Psalm 147:4, KJV). Again, nations and cultures may seem many but they are not as many as the total number of humans on earth – each with his or her own distinct DNA configuration, fingerprint pattern, etc., specially crafted and created by God. They are also not as many as the total number of living creatures on earth, each with its distinct features and functions.

I made these allusions to show you that nations, like other creations of God, do not emerge for the sake of it. As God creates every human to fulfill a specific purpose on earth – confirming this by conferring certain inimitable traits, talents and tendencies on the individual – so also does He create a nation, imbuing it with particular origin, heritage, resources, culture and values, in order to fulfill its calling within the commonwealth of nations around the world.

I like the illustration that Dr. Myles Munroe once gave to prove that God never creates a thing, person or nation without a cause:

God created everything with a purpose in mind, and He also created it with the ability to fulfill its purpose. Everything God has made is the way it is because of why it was created. The 'why' dictates its makeup. The purpose of a thing determines its nature, its design, and its features. You don't make something until you know what you want and why you want it. You'll never find a manufacturer starting a project in a plant, hoping it will turn out to be something useful. Its purpose and design are complete before production starts.

*For example, if a manufacturer decides he wants to build an apparatus that can both record moving pictures onto a magnetic tape for replay and broadcast them live through the medium of television, then he has created a product, a video camera—but the manufacturer designed it first. What's more, everything in the video camera is necessary for its proper functioning. If you could look inside such a camera, you would see things that you didn't know were there and that you don't know the use for. Yet nothing in that product is there for the fun of it. As a matter of fact, because it is so expensive, there had better be nothing in it just for the fun of it.*1

But then, I must still answer the exact question that forms the focus of this chapter: What purpose does God have for creating nations?

GENERAL PURPOSES OF NATIONS

God does not leave us in doubt as to His overall intention in dividing the human race into nations and kingdoms. The Scripture contains the general purposes of God for creating the nations of the world. Let me show you some of them.

1. To explore, exploit and enjoy the bounties of the earth.
"Then God said, "Let Us make man in Our image, according to Our likeness; let them have dominion over the fish of the sea, over the birds of the air, and over the cattle,

over all the earth and over every creeping thing that creeps on the earth." (Genesis 1:26).

Remember that God had created both land and sea, before creating man. Before creating man, He had provided treasures, riches and resources which He had embedded in these creations for man to exploit, maximize and enjoy. These wonderful delights abound in all corners of the earth and only through the notion of nationhood and nationalism can they be exploited.

The point I'm making here is that when nations are formed, people naturally seek to make the best of the resources they have at their disposal. This often leads them to making unprecedented discoveries and realizing boundless possibilities. Take petroleum resources for example. Scientists believe that the geological conditions that would eventually create petroleum formed millions of years ago. This clearly tallies with the idea that petroleum resources, like all other land resources, had been implanted at the time of creation, in certain regions of the world, waiting for exploration by the possessing nations.

2. To show forth His praise.

This is something some people have probably not realized, especially those who despise peoples and cultures that are different from theirs. The diversity that we observe in the cultures, values and resources of the nations of the world, as well as in all other creations of God, serves to reveal the infinite greatness, wisdom, power and majesty of the Almighty God. Romans 1:20 says, **"For since the creation of the world, His invisible attributes are clearly seen, being understood by the things that are made, even His eternal power and Godhead..."**

As I have already shown you in the account of Babel and the children of Noah in the first chapter, God has always wanted diversity, not uniformity, in the races and cultures of human beings.

The reason is simple: Each element of the diversity observed in nature and nations brings glory to Him.

3. To achieve the needed balance in creation.

God, from the beginning, made complementary creations. He created day and night, male and female, summer and winter etc., which serve to complement each other and achieve the needed balance in creation. Even in the Godhead, which is one of the attributes of God revealed in creation (According to Romans 1:21 quoted above) there are three distinct personalities with distinct attributes. Also, in the human entity, there is the body, the soul and the spirit.

In the same way, nations serve to complement each other, while unknowingly fulfilling the ultimate purpose of God for the generality of humanity. There is indeed beauty in diversity! Just try to imagine what this world would look like, if there was no diversity. David P. Murray, in the book, *"The Happy Christian: Ten Ways to be a Joyful Believer in a Gloomy World"*, made this admission:

"Although there's something deep within us that says, The more people are like me, and the more people like me I can gather around me, the happier I'll be, I came to experience the exact opposite. The more I listened, talked, and walked with people of different races, ethnicities, and cultures, the more joy I experienced."[2]

That exactly is one of the general purposes of God for creating nations!

SPECIFIC PURPOSES OF NATIONS

Beyond God's general purposes for creating nations, however, He also has specific reasons for creating each individual nation. What I mean is that each nation has been assigned a definite role to play within the framework of God's ultimate purposes for the nations of the world.

Consider the nation of Israel, for example. It was established by God to be a nation of priests, prophets and patriarchs to the world. God's purpose was for Israel to be a distinct people, a nation that pointed others towards God, His laws, and most importantly, His promised provision of a Redeemer, Messiah, and Savior. Israel was God's "firstborn son" – which should portray the excellence of His holiness and glory.

In this same way, the Scripture contains references to show that nations are established, equipped and sometimes elevated to dominance by God to fulfill specific purposes. As Darris McNeely, in his 2010 narrative, "The Decline and Fall of Nations: A Prophetic Perspective", states:

The Bible is a chronicle of ancient nations that rose and fell according to His plan and purpose. Egypt, Assyria, Babylon, Persia, Greece and Rome—all are mentioned in the narrative. All played key roles in working with the nation of Israel and the Church founded by Jesus Christ. Even today, the lessons of empires embedded in the Bible apply as we watch the modern world move toward what Christ said would be the end of the age.3

From my examination of various biblical and historical narratives, I have found evidences of nations emerging as:

1. Rod of correction/vengeance in the hand of God.
2. Epitome of grandeur and might.
3. Instrument of checkmating excesses of other nations.
4. Cradle of civilization.
5. Mentors in artistry.
6. Leaders in advancement of human rights and dignity.
7. Initiators of innovations.
8. Suppliers of capable labor force.
8. Seedbed of abundant food.
9. Repository of riches.
10. Haven of refuge for the oppressed.

I will be giving more attention to the specific mandates of

nations in the succeeding part of this book. But for now, I must proceed to explain how nations can ascertain the specific callings of God upon them.

CHAPTER THREE

UNLOCKING GOD'S MASTER PLAN FOR EVERY NATION

W̱e now come to a very significant point on our journey to national greatness. How does a nation ascertain its specific calling? A vital question indeed!

To answer this question, it is necessary that I first clarify its essence. Why should nations bother themselves about this quest in the first place? Why should they seek to know their place and purpose in God's grand plan?

I give you these answers:

- Lack of vision leads to lack of direction (Proverbs 29:18). Just as it happens in the lives of individuals, a nation that has no knowledge of the purpose of its existence will wander aimlessly in search of the right direction to follow to achieve greatness.

- Lack of direction leads to lack of focus (Ecclesiastes 10:15). Absence of direction is akin to absence of a goalpost in a football match. What happens to the players? Anything goes. What happens to rules? Everything is allowed. What happens to team-play? Everyone becomes a friend and a foe at the same time. In the end, they are worn out and left wondering why.

- Lack of focus leads to gradual and ultimate destruction (Psalm 107:10-12). The reasons many nations, kingdoms and empires, which were once dominant, became subdued or extinct is because they either lacked focus or lost it along the way.

"The wicked shall be turned into hell, And all the nations that forget God" (Psalm 9:17). Every nation which disregards, despises or deviates from God's purpose for its existence exposes itself to attacks, afflictions and annihilation. The secret of greatness, whether on a personal or national level, lies with God alone; and only by aligning ourselves with His will and purpose can we fulfill the reason for our existence.

So, we return to our question: How does a nation decipher its specific calling?

In Deuteronomy 32:7-8, we are advised to seek wisdom from the fathers so as to discover the purpose of nations.

"Remember the days of old, Consider the years of many generations. Ask your father, and he will show you; your elders, and they will tell you When the Most High divided their inheritance to the nations, When He separated the sons of Adam. He set the boundaries of the peoples according to the number of the children of Israel."

From this Scripture, we realize that there are three important truths we must pay attention to if we are to know the calling and purpose of a nation. Essentially, we can know the calling and purpose of a nation by:

- Retracing its roots
- Revisiting its symbols
- Returning to God and the Scripture

Conscientious application of these keys will guide and galvanize each nation towards discovering and maximizing its potential for matchless greatness.

Let's analyze the keys.

RETRACING THE ROOTS

The very first thing we must do if we wish to find out the calling and purpose of a nation is to remember that both in the heavenly realm and in the physical, there is always a birth date for a nation. Take the United States of America, for instance. Its birthdate was July 4, 1776. For my country Nigeria, it was October 1, 1960.

The Bible adjures us to always go back to the days of the beginning in order to unravel the origin of any nation. Even God, despite His majesty, subjected himself to this rule. In Genesis 1:1, we are told, **"In the beginning God created the heavens and the earth."**

As we can see in this Scripture, God had to go back to the beginning as well, to the days of old, to unveil the purpose of the earth to us in the Holy Scriptures.

What is the significance of this truth to us and our nations today? For every person who wants to discover the purpose and the calling of their nation or country, the first step they must take is to go back to the origins as stated in Deuteronomy 32:7. Such individuals must "remember" the days of old.

In the western part of Nigeria, there is this saying: "If you don't know where you are going, try at least to know where you're coming from." The implication is that where you are coming from should give you a clue to where you are going, or should be going.

Jesus Christ also demonstrated the importance of revisiting the roots of something when He reaffirmed the original plan and blueprint of God for marriage. This happened when the Pharisees came to him, pretentiously seeking to know His view on the subject of divorce. The memorable encounter is recorded in Matthew 19.

"The Pharisees also came to Him, testing Him, and saying to Him, "Is it lawful for a man to divorce his wife for just any reason?" (verse 3).

Jesus, in answering them, made a powerful statement. A statement which not only served to jolt the erring group back to the reality and immutability of God's plan but is apparently also meant to be applied to future groups, especially those in this generation who are frantically seeking to pervert the marriage institution to suit their whims.

"And He answered and said to them, "Have you not read that He who made them AT THE BEGINNING 'made them male and female,'and said, 'For this reason a man shall leave his father and mother and be joined to his wife, and the two shall become one flesh'? So then, they are no longer two but one flesh. Therefore what God has joined together, let not man separate" (verses 4-6, emphasis mine)

Still seeking to validate their perversion, the vain worshippers made reference to the concession seemingly given to them by Moses.

"They said to Him, "Why then did Moses command to give a certificate of divorce, and to put her away?" (verse 7).

Again, Jesus referred them back to the beginning.

"He said to them, "Moses, because of the hardness of your hearts, permitted you to divorce your wives, but FROM THE BEGINNING it was not so"

Jesus Christ simply told them that if they really wanted to

know the mind of God on the institution of marriage, the best thing to do was not to preoccupy themselves with what they considered appropriate or what `Moses was compelled to grant them, but what God originally ordained.

This same principle applies to nations today. To know the purpose of God for our nations, we must go back to the beginnings – we must retrace our roots! As Carl Sandburg once said, "When a nation goes down, or a society perishes, one condition may always be found: they forgot where they came from. They lost sight of what had brought them along."

REVISITING NATIONAL SYMBOLS

"Ask your father, and he will show you; your elders, and they will tell you."

The next thing that the Scripture advises us to do for us to discover the calling and purpose of our nations is to ask questions from those we call the fathers of nations. This is another counsel, resonating with sublime wisdom, from the Holy Writ. There shouldn't be any need to grope in the dark in search of national purpose - simply ask the fathers, the elders who carried the burden for the Independence or founding of the nation. And in what better ways do founding fathers convey their yearnings, visions and aspirations for their nations than through national symbols and documents?

The father or elders are those who carry the burden for the independence of a nation, in some cases for the founding of the nation or, in other cases, they carry the burden for the creation of the nation. Meaning they are much more familiar with the feelings that were associated to the birthing of that country. Moreover they are better exposed to the sentiments and the passions that led to the bringing forth of the nation.

National symbols are easily recognized entities that are used to communicate the history, culture and values of a particular nation. As *Wikipedia*, the online encyclopedia notes, "National symbols intend to unite people by creating visual, verbal, or iconic representations of the national people, values, goals, or history."

In his June 2014 article in the *St. Maarten Island Time*, Fabian Adekunle Badejo explains the essence of national symbols more clearly:

*Symbols are the sometimes cryptic representation of a people's values, ideals, and aspirations. They are the morse codes by which our history, culture, and highest achievements are transmitted. No society can function properly without its own set of symbols because they are the focal point around which the people are united. To the extent to which those symbols are valued, to that same extent would members of that society feel a sense of belonging, of kinship, of even patriotism.*1

Gabriella Elgenius, in 2005, went even further by saying:

*National symbols and ceremonies form a central part of a 'secular' religion which provides anchorage in a dynamic world. National symbols and ceremonies also have an effect upon the community they represent; that is, they raise collective consciousness of 'who we are' and 'where we are from'.*2

Founding fathers are much more familiar with the feelings associated with the birthing of a nation. They are better exposed to the sentiments and yearnings that led to the bringing forth of the nation. As a result, the symbols, declarations, documents and landmarks that they instituted or inspired must be taken seriously.

National symbols have deep spiritual implications. It is always the workings of God to cause elders to come together and release some thoughts that carry His mind, wishes, purposes and callings for a particular nation.

John 1:1 says, **"In the beginning was the Word, and the Word was with God, and the Word was God."**

Please note that words are expressions of thoughts. In this case, the words are thoughts of God. These thoughts of God are what God places upon the heart of people He put as the progenitors and originators of a nation. These people conceive in their minds and in their hearts, thoughts that were planted into them by God. These people are later known as the founding fathers of a nation, while the thoughts that are given birth to through them become the documents upon which the nation is built. The American Declaration of Independence is a good example of this.

In some other cases these thoughts are recorded in the national pledge or national anthem. Indeed, there are various means and ways whereby divinely conceived burdens and thoughts are reproduced into documents. Yet in some cases these burdens could find their expressions in national documents like the constitution.

A careful examination of those original thoughts, words and documents will always reveal the calling and reason for the creation of every nation. Study, research and analyze carefully the early documents. There you will discover the purpose for the creation of your nation.

National symbols consist mainly of the national flag, the national colors, the coat of arms and the national anthem. In some cases however it could also include the national pledge, the national animal, the national bird, the national tree, the national flower, the national fruit, as well as national landmarks of historical importance.

Very interestingly, the history of national symbols dates back to the Bible. For instance, following the miraculous crossing of the River Jordan, the Israelites were asked to set up a memorial for future generations. Joshua 4:5-12 says:

"And Joshua said to them, "Pass on before the ark of the Lord your God into the midst of the Jordan, and take up each of you a stone upon his shoulder, according to the number of the tribes of the people of Israel, that this may be a sign

among you. **When your children ask in time to come, 'What do those stones mean to you?' then you shall tell them that the waters of the Jordan were cut off before the ark of the covenant of the Lord. When it passed over the Jordan, the waters of the Jordan were cut off. So these stones shall be to the people of Israel a memorial forever."'**

If God could suggest and approve of the setting up of this memorial landmark for the Israelites, it is because He knows that a careful examination of national symbols, documents and landmarks will always reveal His calling upon every nation. Burdens, symbols and documents are of great importance. So also are the burden carriers, the fathers, the elders - to connect us to what they felt, how they felt and their visions for our nations. When we succeed in reconnecting back to those original intents and purposes both through documents and symbols, then we are at the root of our nation's calling and purpose.

This is one of the main reasons why history matters. In our schools, from primary to tertiary institutions, we often hear of History as a subject, but unfortunately few truly know the meaning and significance of history in national development (I will, in a later chapter of this book, dwell extensively on the place of History in preservation and dissemination of national values).

I think at this point it might be interesting for you to know how God transmits His will and purpose into the hearts of the founders of nations.

In Matthew 16:17-19,we are told: **"Jesus answered and said to him, "Blessed are you, Simon Bar-Johnah, for flesh and blood has not revealed this to you, but My Father who is in heaven. And I also say to you that you are Peter, and on this rock I will build my church, and the gates of Hades shall not prevail against it. And I will give you the keys of the kingdom of heaven, and whatever you bind on earth will**

be bound in heaven, and whatever you loose on earth will be loosed in heaven."

The preceding story to this declaration by Jesus is that Jesus, together with his disciples, had entered into a region called Caesarea Philippi. This was a new territory for Him. The people of the land did not know much of Him because His ministry had been in other parts of the nation. On getting to this new territory, Jesus decided to use it as an illustrated teaching for His disciples. Jesus would normally use the natural things of life to teach deep spiritual lessons.

At the end of the day, the disciples discovered that none of them could actually give the right answer to the question of Jesus, "Who do men say that I, the Son of Man, am?" some of the disciples had suggested that he was being seen as John the Baptist or Elijah, Jeremiah or some other prophet. After numerous failed attempts of the disciples to second guess who He was, something happened out of the ordinary, completely unexpected: Simon Peter suddenly gave the right answer, "You are the Christ, the Son of the living God."

Jesus immediately seized the opportunity and made the record straight that this was not an answer given from the understanding of Peter. In other words, this was something beyond Peter. Jesus answered and said to him, "Blessed are you, Simon Bar-Johnah, for flesh and blood has not revealed this to you, but My Father who is in heaven. And I also say to you that you are Peter, and on this rock I will build my church, and the gates of Hades shall not prevail against it."

In the story above, God was setting up His disciples for the new thing He wanted. God wanted to give birth to the church, and as with every other thing that is given birth to from heaven on the earth, God needed a human instrument who would conceive the thoughts and later release the words upon which the church, nation or structure would be built.

It is this same algorithm and formula that still obtains today. Nations included. Whenever God wants to give birth to a nation or anything new on the earth, He triggers corresponding events just like we saw above with the question, "who do men say that I am?"

God, in His infinite wisdom, often allows human efforts and attempts to accomplish His purposes in the physical to fail. This is evident in the illustration above. The disciples were trying to give the answer to Jesus' question in their own understanding and efforts, they failed. The answers they gave did not correspond with the truth.

The same process happens when a nation is been given birth to - many fight, struggle and die in the process. In the aftermath of human failures and casualties, God now allows for other men to arise upon whose hearts he impresses his burdens, that are eventually translated into words that later become documents in various forms.

It is now upon those words of revelations that nations are built, just like we could see in the story above. Jesus said, **"On this rock I would build my church"** the rock being the words of revelation that Peter pronounced. In a similar vein today, every nation is always built upon some words which are documented in different formats.

In many cases, unfortunately, these fathers of nations would naively think that they are the ones who in their wisdom were able to create or give birth to a nation. Peter was lucky because Jesus was standing by him to correct that erroneous notion. His words were very corrective **"for flesh and blood has not revealed this to you but my father who is in heaven."**

Thanks to the Holy Scriptures, we too could be shielded from that kind of erroneous thinking as we read Scriptures like

Deuteronomy 32:7-8. We can clearly hear the words of God the father. So, I repeat, if you really to know God's purpose for your nation, don't rely on your understanding, go to the days of old, ask your fathers and elders and through them you will know the way. Purposes, intents shall be revealed to you as it was also in their time revealed to them by the God of nations.

RETURNING TO GOD AND THE SCRIPTURE

"When the Most High divided their inheritance to the nations, When He separated the sons of Adam. He set the boundaries of the peoples according to the number of the children of Israel" (Deuteronomy 32:8).

From this passage it is clear that it is God who designs every nation's boundaries. God is at the foundation of every nation. He measures out to every nation their boundaries and their callings. This is understandable since it is only the creator of a thing that can tell or reveal the purpose for it. God is the creator of all things including nations; He knows the reasons and explanations behind the creation of every nation.

The implication of this is that, for us to discover the calling of a nation, we must acknowledge the boundless power and supremacy of the omniscient God in the formation, composition and direction of every nation. With this acknowledgement comes the understanding that neither circumstances nor men, in themselves, trigger the birth of a nation, but the invisible hand of God which nudges men and orchestrates events towards the actualization of His eternal purpose. This understanding should inevitably propel us to seek God's face in ascertaining His desire for our nation.

What every wise person does when a product or device proves too complex to operate is to consult the manufacturer or the provided manual for the product. This underscores the indispensability of God's Word in the discovery of national purpose. It may sound incredible, but the Bible actually contains vital revelations to stir and steer every nation towards the discovery and fulfillment of its destiny. This fact will be fully explored in the succeeding part of the book.

Dr. Myles Munroe once gave an explanation on the importance of seeking God to ascertain purpose:

"If you want to know the purpose of something, don't ask the thing itself. Why? It didn't plan, design, or build itself. Only the manufacturer knows the why and how of his product; no one else truly does. That is why he can claim perfect relationship with his product. Therefore, if you're going to use something, the first question you need to ask is, —Who made this? If you buy a certain kind of guitar, you need to consult the manufacturer who made that particular guitar. That is why the company includes an instructional booklet with the instrument; the booklet tells you how to use the guitar based on its purpose. You don't use it to paddle a boat. You don't use it to play baseball. In other words, the manufacturer sent you the manual to protect you from abusing the product and so you could have the full enjoyment of it."

A good example of how God could be wisely consulted concerning the destiny of a nation is contained in Genesis 25:21-23. When Rebekah, the wife of Isaac, began to experience some discomfort with her pregnancy, she did a remarkable thing and got a memorable result:

"Now Isaac pleaded with the Lord for his wife, because she was barren; and the Lord granted his plea, and Rebekah his wife conceived. But the children struggled together within her; and she said, "If all is well, why am I like this?" So she went to inquire of the Lord. And the Lord said to her: "Two nations are in your womb, Two peoples shall be separated from your body;

One people shall be stronger than the other, And the older shall serve the younger."

There and then, Rebekah got to know the cause of her discomfort and the fate of the children in her womb. She went on to have Esau – the progenitor of the Edomites, and Jacob – the patriarch of the Israelites.

The role of the Scripture in directing or redirecting the destiny of a nation is equally demonstrated in 2 Kings 22 and 23. The Book of the Law that had been long abandoned by the people of Judah was stumbled upon by Hilkiah, the high priest, in the temple and sent to King Josiah. The reading of the contents opened the eyes of the king to the dreadful realization that the nation had long deviated from its calling and was on the brink of destruction.

That discovery led to the floodgates of reforms that Josiah unleashed on the entire nation in a bid to get them back on the right track. How many nations of the world today are wallowing in the darkness of misery and misfortune, simply because they have relegated the Word of Light to the background in their affairs!

APPLICATION OF THE KEYS

Throughout the chapters in the next part of the book, detailed attention will be given to practical applications of the three keys discussed here. The purpose of God for some selected countries will thus be unraveled. The essence is to demonstrate the efficacy of the combination of these keys in ascertaining the specific calling of God upon every nation of the world.

As we embark on these practical applications, it is my prayer that through my efforts in this book, never again will a nation of the world be left in the dark as to its place, purpose and predestination in the master plan of the Almighty!

PART TWO

UNRAVELLING THE CALLINGS OF SPECIFIC NATIONS

CHAPTER FOUR

UNITED STATES OF AMERICA: THE NATION IN A RENDEZVOUS WITH DESTINY

The United States of America is currently regarded as the world's sole superpower nation due to its matchless prominence in international relations and global influence. In all dimensions of state power, including geography, economic resources, military might, diplomacy and national identity, the nation remains the unchallenged world leader. Consequently, every part of the world has come under the purview of its interests.

The magnitude of the United States' influence in the world is indeed phenomenal. Writing for the Forbes magazine in November 2013, Johnathan Adelman of the Josef Korbel School of International Studies at the University of Denver, explains some key details of the United States' superpower status:

"The United States leads the world in high technology (Silicon Valley), finance and business (Wall Street), the movies (Hollywood) and higher education (17 of the top 20 universities in the world in Shanghai's Jaotong

University survey). The United States has a First World trade profile (massive exports of consumer and technology goods and imports of natural resources). It is still the world's leader for FDI at 180 billion dollars, almost twice its nearest competitor. The United States, spending 560 billion dollars a year, has the most powerful military in the world. Its GDP (16 trillion dollars) is more than twice the size of China's GDP. As the first new nation, it has the world's longest functioning democracy in a world filled with semi-democratic or non-democratic countries. Its stock market, at an all time high, still reflects American leadership of the global economy."1

However, the emergence of the United States as the sole superpower is one that still surprises many people, considering the imperial struggle for dominance between it and two other nations that were considered superpowers for the most part of the last hundred years: the United Kingdom and the Soviet Union (USSR). As Tom Engelhardt of *TomDispatch* once wrote, "Never before had a single power of such stature, wealth and military clout been left so triumphantly solitary, without the hint of a serious challenger anywhere."2

Given the extent of the struggle that once existed among the erstwhile rival nations and the fact that within the period before the Second World War, the United States had not yet mastered all the various dimensions of state power, one would not have imagined that the nation would occupy its current position. Yet it does. But as every discerning mind in the world can attest, the emergence of America to the Eldorado of global prominence is not by ordinary orchestration or man-made permutations. There seems to be a manifestation of divine predestination at work.

Let me prove this with facts.

First, we must ask: What weakened the competitive powers of the other nations with whom the United States previously struggled for dominance? Was it any particular maneuvering or spectacular machination from the United States itself? Not at all.

The first factor in the ascendancy was the devastation wrought on Great Britain by the Second World War and the Suez Crisis (1956) respectively. These historic events effectively saw the elimination of the United Kingdom from the roll call of superpowers.

In a report titled, "Britain and World War II" the *Daily Mail* of the United Kingdom stated in 2006: "World War II sealed the fate of the British Empire, though the United Kingdom had begun loosening control over its empire earlier."3 The same report added that while "the war had shattered the United Kingdom's economy…the United States and the Soviet Union came out of the war as the world's most powerful nations."

Further on the surprisingly positive effect of the war on the United States, Mamta Aggarwal, in his article, "How USA Became the Only Superpower of the World", said: "The Second World War had done no damage to the US economy. In fact, the problems created by the Great Depression had been overcome during the war. The post-war period was one of unprecedented economic prosperity. From 1940 to 1987, the GNP rose from about $ 100 billion to about $ 5,200 billion while the population rose from about 132 million to about 240 million. The affluence of the American people was reflected in the growth of what is usually described as "consumer culture" or "consumerism"."

Following the elimination of the United Kingdom, the United States had only the Soviet Union to contend with. Interestingly no one could have foretold which of these nations would subdue the other because of their seemingly equally formidable capabilities. According to Engelhardt (quoted earlier), the two nations were "so stunningly mighty and over-armed—great inland empires—that, unlike previous powers, they could not even imagine how to wage war directly upon each other, not without obliterating much of civilization. The full planet nonetheless became their battlefield in what was known as the Cold War only because hot ones were banished to "the peripheries" and the conflict took place, in part, in "the shadows"

Then something unexpected happened. In December of 1991, the world watched in utter amazement as the Soviet Union literally crumbled like a house of cards, disintegrating into fifteen separate countries. Like a daydream that suddenly became a reality, the United States was astounded to see its previously fearsome enemy suddenly brought to its knees, without any physical blow.

And thus the United States emerged, almost effortlessly, as the grand spectacle of power, grandeur and veneration for the world!

IS THERE NOT A CAUSE?

This notable question, posed by David in the Bible to his brother in 1 Samuel 17:29 aptly applies to the American situation. David had been divinely led, through the assignment given to him by his father, to the battlefield where the Israelites had been cowering before Goliath, the giant of Gath. It was not his intention to be at such a place at that time; but God who had a definite purpose for His life had ordained it that he should be strategically led thus, so his ultimate destiny could begin to manifest.

Whether consciously or unconsciously, David affirmed this providential undercurrent when his eldest brother, Eliab, accused him of insolence and pride for coming to the battleground. His answer was: **"What have I done now? Is there not a cause?"**

Let's bring this home, and ask: Is there not a cause for the providential rise of the United States to being an unchallenged superpower? To what purpose has God thus exalted America to the pinnacle of excellence and influence? Is it, as it currently seems, to be at the forefront of promoting decadence, perversions, immoralities, pseudo-Christianity, anti-God campaigns, trampling on sovereignties, disregard for authorities (UN), toppling of governments, backing of "useful" dictators, paranoid snooping, clandestine wars and economic oppression?

What exactly is God's purpose for America? What should the nation be doing with all the privileges, resources and capabilities that the Almighty has freely bestowed on it? Let's unravel the answers with our keys.

RETRACING THE ROOTS OF THE UNITED STATES

Most people trace the birth of the Unites States of America as a nation to July 4, 1776 when colonists in the Thirteen American Colonies officially declared their Independence from the British monarchy and aristocracy. However, not many know the events that led to that celebrated moment, or the fact that the agitation for absolute self-governance had begun long before then.

To understand the roots of the United States, we have to look deeper into the origins and cultures of the Thirteen Colonies and make cogent observations. The Thirteen Colonies, by the way, were: Delaware, Pennsylvania, New Jersey, Georgia, Connecticut, Massachusetts Bay, Maryland, South Carolina, New Hampshire, Virginia, Province of New York, Province of North Carolina, and Colony of Rhode Island and Providence Plantations. The States of Massachusetts, Rhode Island, Connecticut, and New Jersey were formed by mergers of previous colonies.

The first observation one immediately makes is the beautiful diversity and intermingling of cultures. Early settlers and colonists in what became known as the United States came from different parts of Europe – Sweden, Finland, France, Spain, Great Britain and the Netherlands. Thus, there were the Dutch of New Netherland, the Swedes and Finns of New Sweden, the English Quakers of Pennsylvania, the English Puritans of New England, the English settlers of Jamestown, and the "worthy poor" of Georgia. Each of these groups came, settled and built colonies with distinctive social, religious, political and economic styles. In the course of time, however, the British, with their superior might and resources, were able to subdue other settlers and the entire colonies came under the control of Britain.

The second and indeed the most important observation is that the early settlers were predominantly practicing Christians. In fact, a considerable number of them were men and women who, in the face of religious persecution, refused to compromise and passionately held their Christian convictions. Their mission was thus to seek a place where they could worship God freely. Most of the early British settlers in particular, came with the aim of reforming the Church of England by creating a new, pure church in the New World. As the *Wikipedia* notes "They fled England and in America attempted to create a "nation of saints" or a "City upon a Hill": an intensely religious, thoroughly righteous community designed to be an example for all of Europe."5

Beginning with the Pilgrim settlers who had settled in Massachusetts as early as 1620, other settlers came with different denominations of Christianity. The Puritans came from England in 1620 and settled in New England and as far as the West Indies. Both the Spanish and the French also set up Catholic missions, churches and institutions in Maryland, California and New Orleans respectively.

Interestingly, some of the colonies were actually founded by clergymen with religious intents. Notable among these are Pennsylvania and Rhode Island. Rhode Island was founded by Roger Williams, an English Protestant theologian, in 1636. His goal was to establish a settlement, where people could practice the Christian religion without state interference. He named his first settlement, *Providence*, in recognition of "God's merciful Providence", which he believed was responsible for revealing such a haven for him and his followers to settle. Providence remains the capital and most populous city in Rhode Island today. The question however is, is the vision of this founding father still being maintained?

Pennsylvania was also founded in 1862 by William Penn, as an American state run under Quaker principles. This provided opportunity for Quakers who had been persecuted for their religious beliefs to settle in a place where they could worship freely. Other dissenters from the established churches also migrated to Pennsylvania. Many of them practiced brands of Christianity disfavored by the government of their homelands. Huguenots (from France), Puritans, Catholics, and Calvinists all migrated to Pennsylvania.

Now, this is really important – and should put paid to the argument that America was not founded on Christian beliefs. By the year 1702 many of all 13 American colonies had some form of state-supported brand of Christianity. Those who had no official Christian denomination had, like all other colonies, direct references to God, Christianity and religion, in either their charters or constitutions.

The third observation in the colonists was their unmistakable commitment to justice, liberty and rights of man. This has always been in the consciousness of the United States of America, beginning with the colonies. Indeed, the control of the British Empire over the colonies was both minimal and fragile. And even then, the inhabitants of the colonies were still not satisfied with the fact that the British took advantage of them by meddling in their affairs, imposing taxes on them, and refusing them representation in the British parliament. They couldn't stand such injustice.

As early as the 1750s, they had begun collaborating with each other to devise ways of severing ties with the British (see the Albany Congress of 1754 for example). Leaders, such as Benjamin Franklin of Pennsylvania, saddled themselves with the responsibility of promoting a sense of American identity, which further heightened the yearning of the people for independence.

The passion for liberty and self-determination was so strong within the colonies that drumbeats of war against the British were already being beaten years before the eventual declaration of independence. One of those who loudly conveyed the heartbeat of the Americans was Patrick Henry, a great orator and an important figure in the history of the revolution that sounded the death knell for British control over the colonies. On March 23, 1775, as the colonists assembled at the Virginia Convention, debating whether to mobilize forces against the British, Henry gave the rousing speech, "Give Me Liberty Or Give Me Death". He concluded it thus:

The war is actually begun! The next gale that sweeps from the north will bring to our ears the clash of resounding arms! Our brethren are already in the field! Why stand we here idle? What is it that gentlemen wish? What would they have? Is life so dear, or peace so sweet, as to be purchased at the price of chains and slavery? Forbid it, Almighty God! I know not what course others may take; but as for me, give me liberty or give me death!

Sentiments for liberty continued to mount so strongly in the colonies and by June 11, 1776, when the Colonies' Second Continental Congress met in Philadelphia, their minds were made up: It's Independence or nothing. They consequently formed a committee whose express purpose was drafting a document that would formally express their yearnings as they severed their ties with Great Britain. Thomas Jefferson, who was considered the most eloquent writer among the committee members, was assigned to compose the initial document. Changes were made to the draft and the Continental Congress officially adopted the final version on July 4, 1776.

And thus marked the birth of the United States of America!

In the next section of this chapter, I will be taking a closer look at the Declaration of Independence to reveal some salient truths about the calling and values of the United States. But we must first reflect on the lessons from the roots of the nation and compare the beginnings to the present day. America was actually founded on the primary principles of perpetuating the gospel of Christ, propagating righteousness, promoting justice and ensuring that the basic rights of man are guaranteed, provided that such rights are exercised within the ambits of the Laws of God, on which the constitution is based.

REVISITING THE NATIONAL SYMBOLS OF THE UNITED STATES

As I previously noted, the burdens, aspirations and values of the founding founders of a nation are usually transmitted through the national symbols, landmarks and documents bequeathed to the future generations. What then are the national symbols of the United States and what messages do they convey?

The national symbols of the United States consist of:
- The Flag of the United States
- Seal of the United States
- National animal/bird: Bald eagle
- National anthem: "The Star-Spangled Banner"
- National mottos: "In God We Trust"
- National floral emblem: Rose
- National march: "The Stars and Stripes Forever"
- National creed: American's Creed
- National tree: Oak

Analyzing the deep meanings and messages embedded in each of these symbols will take a whole book; but I will endeavor to focus on the first three because I believe there is so much in them that can echo what is in the rest. However before I do the analyses of the significance of these symbols, let me quickly revisit

America's most cherished symbol of liberty, the Declaration of Independence.

One thing I find really fascinating about the Declaration is the introduction. Here, the founding fathers ensure that their motive for establishing the nation is unequivocally defined. The Declaration begins thus:

"When in the Course of human events, it becomes necessary for one people to dissolve the political bands which have connected them with another, and to assume among the powers of the earth, the separate and equal station to which the Laws of Nature and of Nature's God entitle them, a decent respect to the opinions of mankind requires that they should declare the causes which impel them to the separation."

Thereafter, they begin their explanation:

We hold these truths to be self-evident, that all men are created equal, that they are endowed by their Creator with certain unalienable Rights, that among these are Life, Liberty and the pursuit of Happiness.--That to secure these rights, Governments are instituted among Men, deriving their just powers from the consent of the governed, --That whenever any Form of Government becomes destructive of these ends, it is the Right of the People to alter or to abolish it, and to institute new Government, laying its foundation on such principles and organizing its powers in such form, as to them shall seem most likely to effect their Safety and Happiness...

One other thing that strikes me, which, oddly enough, many do not pay attention to is a sentence contained in the second to the last paragraph. In that paragraph, the founding fathers stated all the steps they had taken to ensure that the ties that bound them to Britain were not forcefully truncated, but which were not heeded. The paragraph reads:

"Nor have We been wanting in attentions to our Brittish brethren. We have warned them from time to time of attempts by their legislature to extend an unwarrantable jurisdiction over us. We have reminded them of the circumstances of our emigration and settlement here. We have appealed to

*their native justice and magnanimity, and we have conjured them by the ties
of our common kindred to disavow these usurpations, which, would inevitably
interrupt our connections and correspondence. They too have been deaf to the
voice of justice and of consanguinity…"*

The statement I'm referring to is: *"We have reminded them [the
British] of the circumstances of our emigration and settlement here."*

This statement not only expresses a key reason for breaking
free but also shows just how focused they wished to be in
sticking to their original calling and fulfilling their destiny. The
said "circumstances" as disclosed by their charters, constitutions
and other historical records have been sufficiently explored in the
above section. The summary is: They wanted to be free to pursue
their interests (especially in devoting themselves to God without
restraints and pursuing true happiness). They wanted to be bound
by no other law, other than the law of God and that which they
devised as an application and amplification of the divine law.

My concern, which I believe equally echoes the mind of God,
is, hundreds of years on, do Americans still think of the aspiration
of these founding fathers? "If we ever forget that we are One
Nation Under God, then we will be a nation gone under," said
Ronald Reagan.

ANALYZING THE SYMBOLS
1. The Flag of the United States

The American flag is popularly believed to have been designed
by Elizabeth Griscom Ross in June 1776. One year later, in June
14, 1777, the Continental Congress passed the first Flag Act, which
said that the flag would be made up of thirteen alternating red and
white stripes and thirteen white stars on a blue field. The thirteen
stars represented the original thirteen colonies that made up the
United States. Thus, stars have been added to the flag as new states
join the union. Currently, the flag contains 50 stars. However the

stripes remain thirteen to continue to reflect the original thirteen colonies.

I will be talking more about the significance of the colors white, red and blue in the flag, while analyzing the second symbol – the Great Seal. However, let me say that it is not in vain that while stars continue to be added to the flag, the original thirteen stripes remain unchanged. This, I believe, is intended to serve as a constant reminder of the origins of the United States and particularly the goals, yearning and aspirations of the colonists and the founding fathers.

2. The Seal of the United States

The Great Seal is the official emblem of the United States. From the year 1782, the U.S. government has been authenticating official documents with the seal. Beyond that, the obverse (front) of the seal is used as the national coat of arms of the United States. It is officially used on documents such as United States passports, military insignia, embassy placards, and various flags. What makes this necessary? The answer lies in the significant symbolism of the seal.

A website dedicated to this momentous symbol aptly describes it as "the eloquent device designed by America's founders to convey their vision to the world and to the future."7 Explaining further, it says, "…the two sides of the Great Seal embody the essential guiding principles these farsighted patriots hoped we would always follow."

What then are these principles? Let's extract them from the components of the seal.

3. The Bald Eagle

Since the bald eagle is in itself a national symbol of the United States, I will be discussing the details of its symbolism later. But here, in the Great Seal, the eagle is seen with its wings outstretched. In its right talon, which is the stronger talon, it holds an olive branch, which symbolizes the power of peace. In its left talon is a bundle of 13 arrows. While the number 13 refers to the original states, the arrows depict power of war.

Taken together, the message in both talons is that the United States has "a strong desire for peace, but will always be ready for war." But more significantly is the fact that the eagle has its head turned towards the olive branch, on its right side. It is a message the founding fathers wished to convey that the United States should make the pursuit of peace its primary focus in all things. War must come only as a last resort, when every attempt with the power of peace seems to have failed.

In the eagle's beak is a scroll with the motto *E pluribus unum* (Latin for "Out of Many, One"). Charles Thomson, who designed the final seal, explained that the motto alludes to the union between the states and federal government.

4. The Shield

The shield lies on the chest of the eagle. It is composed of seven white (argent) stripes, six red (gules) stripes, and a blue (azure) top section (Chief). According to the official explanation given for the design, The shield is composed of the blue Chief (top horizontal bar) and the red and white Pales (thirteen vertical stripes) which represent the several states all joined in one solid compact entire, supporting a Chief which unites the whole and represents Congress. The motto, mentioned above, alludes to this union.

The stripes are kept closely united by the Chief, and the Chief depends upon the union and the strength resulting from it for its support to denote the Confederacy of the United States of America and the preservation of their union through Congress.

The most striking feature and significance of the shield lies in the fact that it is attached to the eagle without any form of support. Explaining this, Charles Thomson said: "The Escutcheon [shield] is born on the breast of an American Eagle without any other supporters, to denote that the United States of America ought to rely on their own Virtue."

What message is here for America? By upholding virtue, not vice, it makes itself invulnerable and invincible to external attacks and aggressions. America currently seems to be agitated and paranoid because the shield of virtue bequeathed to it by the founding fathers is weakened, if not completely replaced with the veneer of vice. No wonder its case has become like that of Israel, of whom the Scripture says, **"Israel hath cast off the thing that is good: the enemy shall pursue him"** (Romans 8:3, KJV).

5. Stars

In the words of Charles Thomson, the constellation of stars above the head of the eagle, "denotes a new State taking its place and rank among other sovereign powers." Today, America has, through divine help, gone beyond taking its rank among sovereign states to actually taking the lead above them all.

It is equally interesting to note that the stars in the seal are enveloped by a glory, a heraldic term for an emanation of light rays, usually golden color. This is the only symbolic element that appears on both sides of the Great Seal. The official explanation is that the glory symbolizes the light of Providence (God). This, together with the eye and motto *Annuit Coeptis* (on the reverse side of the seal) allude to the many signal interpositions of God in favor of the American cause. *Annuit Coeptis* means "He (God) has favored our undertakings."

The founding fathers of America obviously considered the consent of God to be indispensable in their undertakings. Does

America still uphold the same belief in its dealings with its people and other nations?

6. Unfinished Pyramid

This is conspicuously depicted on the reverse side of the seal. Charles Thomson pointed out that "The pyramid signifies strength and duration." It is believed that the inspiration was derived from the Great Pyramids of Egypt.

It is noteworthy that the capstone that should have completed the pyramid is also portrayed, but not joined to the main body of the pyramid. In this capstone lies the eye of Providence. Two things can be deduced from the manner in which the pyramid is presented. On the one hand is the paramount need for the decisive input of God in the actualization of the American dream. Without God, the efforts of the founding fathers would never lead America to its ultimate destiny.

On the other hand is an important fact stated by one of the founding fathers, Thomas Jefferson, and which every American must heed today:

"The generation which commences a revolution rarely completes it."

The founding fathers have laid a solid foundation for the nation of America. What (and how) is the present generation building on it? Are efforts being made to work towards perfecting the good work begun centuries ago or is the present generation simply perverting it with godless choices?

7. The Colors

Three colors are depicted on both the shield in the seal, as well as the flag of the United States. These colors constitute a banner which the Unites States wears as a reflection and projection of its core values and ideals. According to the founding fathers, the color white signifies purity, cleanness of life and rectitude of conduct; red signifies valor and bravery; while blue signifies vigilance, perseverance, and justice.

Once again, we're reminded of the calling of America and the vision of the founding fathers – the pursuit of godliness (purity and innocence), of excellence (valor and bravery) and of justice.

8. The Bald Eagle

The bald eagle was chosen June 20, 1782 as the emblem of the United States because of its long life, great strength and majestic looks. Most importantly, the eagle represents freedom, vision and excellence. According to Maude M. Grant, "The eagle, full of the boundless spirit of freedom, living above the valleys, strong and powerful in his might, has become the national emblem of a country that offers freedom in word and thought and an opportunity for a full and free expansion into the boundless space of the future."

Like the eagle, America was conceived as a nation that pursues grand principles, not base passions. A nation that uses its boundless freedom to act as a pacesetter in excellence, not a trend-setter in decadence. Let America think!

MESSAGE FOR THE UNITED STATES FROM THE SCRIPTURE

Could there be a direct message for the American nation from God? The answer is Yes. Hidden in the Scripture is an express admonition that applies to no other nation on earth more than the United States. Before I point it out, let me provide a little background.

From our exploration of the calling of America so far, one

distinguishing trait has been established about this significant nation from its beginnings to date – its love of LIBERTY! America is a nation that prides itself on liberty. One of the founding fathers, Thomas Jefferson, went as far as to describe America as an "empire of liberty"; while the national anthem expressly describes the nation as "the land of the free." And as if to physically establish, underline and propagate this ideal, there is a colossal sculpture called "The Statue of Liberty" on Liberty Island in New York Harbor in New York City, in the United States.

So, what message or mandate does God have for this Land of the Free? It is found in 1 Peter 2:16: **"As free, yet not using liberty as a cloak for vice, but as bondservants of God"**

Can anyone be in doubt that while this verse had an immediate application to the believers to whom it was first addressed, it also had a prophetic reference to the nation of America? All that such a skeptic (if there is any at all) needs is to revisit the aspirations of the founding fathers of America as has been exhaustively highlighted here and compare them with the admonition of this verse.

Once again, what was the motive of the majority of the first settlers in the United States? Freedom from tyrannical monarchs and despotic priests. What did they intend to do with their freedom? To devote themselves to God – to serve God freely, without slavish conformity to dogmas and decrees.

Obviously, the founding fathers were inspired and led by God to fulfill this very mandate. And, truly, they were passionate about keeping to this calling. This passion, as has been already proved from the Declaration, was a key motivation for their Independence from Britain. Centuries on, however, what is America doing with its freedom? Practicing and projecting virtue or producing and promoting vice?

LET AMERICA REFLECT!

CHAPTER FIVE

NIGERIA: THE BLESSED GIANT WITH A THINKING PROBLEM

S uppose one were to doubt the fact that God has special interests and purposes for nations of the world, I believe such doubts would melt away as soon as such a person decides to beam his searchlight on Nigeria. The circumstances that surrounded Nigeria's birth, the extraordinary events that shaped and continue to shape its history, the multiplicity of its cultures, the peculiarities of its people, the vastness of its resources, the undulations of its reputation, the prophecies and projections that have been made concerning it, as well as its strategic position among the nations of the world – all attest to the fact that this nation occupies a special position in God's program for the world.

Currently, with a population of over 170 million people, the country is not only the most populous nation in Africa and the 7th most populous in the world but also the most populous Black nation on earth. It also has one of the highest populations of youths in the world, numbering over 60 million. Beyond that, Nigeria is the largest economy in Africa. In addition, it is considered a regional superpower, contributing massively to peacekeeping missions in the continent.

Let me narrow my focus on the socio-cultural composition of Nigeria because therein lies one of the strongest indicators of the fact that the nation indeed has a special place in destiny. Inhabited by over 500 ethnic groups, who speak different languages, the country is viewed as a multinational state. And then there is the unique religious configuration, with the country being divided roughly in half between Christians, who live mostly in the southern and central parts of the country, and Muslims in the northern and southwestern regions.

The ethno-religious and other seeming intractable differences between the Northern and Southern parts of the nation have formed the backgrounds for ceaseless tensions, sporadic conflicts, secession-attempts and an outright civil war – leading many to believe that the 1914 amalgamation of the Southern and Northern protectorates by Britain to form the nation now called Nigeria was a huge mistake. Amazingly, however, every attempt to undo this "forced union" by breaking up the nation has proved futile. Every inter-ethnic or religious conflict seems to end up strengthening the cords that bind the nation together. What's more, every projection of breakup by "seasoned" observers and historians has proved null and void.

Election periods, in particular, often prove significant for doomsayers and their bewilderment with the state of affairs in Nigeria. Predictions of implosion are often rife. For instance, just before the 2011 elections, Former U.S. Ambassador to Nigeria, John Campbell, wrote an alarming article that was published in the September/October web edition of the Foreign Affairs journal. Titled "Nigeria on the Brink: What Happens If the 2011 Elections Fail?", part of the article read:

"The 2011 elections in Nigeria, scheduled for January 22, pose a threat to the stability of the United States' most important partner in West Africa.

The end of a power-sharing arrangement between the Muslim North and the Christian South, as now seems likely, could lead to post-election sectarian violence, paralysis of the executive branch, and even a coup…Nigerians have long danced on the edge of the cliff without falling off. Yet at this juncture, the odds are not good for a positive outcome, and it is difficult to see how Nigeria can move back from the brink."1

But then, Nigeria did actually move back from the brink – if ever it was there – as it had always seemed to do after all negative predictions.

Again, just before the 2015 elections, both the print and the electronic media were awash with chilling reports and frightening forecasts. In fact, to many, if Nigeria had proved to be a cat with nine lives in the past, refusing to collapse despite all predictions, then the 2015 elections were likely to sound the ultimate death knell for it. On November 8, 2012, Bayo Fapounda wrote in the Punch newspaper:

"As the country approaches a century of nationhood, it is ironical that instead of celebrating the birth of a nation and a shared destiny, there are latent fears that the "mistake of 1914" may manifest in the break-up of the country in 2015 - a year after the centenary date. Will Nigeria as we know it today cease to exist in 2015 as predicted? Will the country implode and eventually be balkanized to reflect the years after amalgamation? Can the country continue to exist under this present warped federal structure?"

Yet, the elections came and went, without much ado. In fact, the presidential election not only proved to be one of the best elections ever held in the country - it actually set the record as being the first election in which an incumbent president would be unseated by an opposition candidate. Interestingly, through it all, the nation remains intact, if not invincible.

So, let's ask ourselves: Exactly what sustains this nation and proves the best of analysts to be liars? Ironically, even John Campbell who predicted doom for Nigeria before the 2011 elections made an observation which should have actually caused him to think twice before writing off the nation as a goner. Let me extract a line from his quote above:

"Nigerians have long danced on the edge of the cliff without falling off."

This, unknown to Mr. Campbell, aptly highlights one of the marvels that characterize Nigeria as one with a divine mandate. Compare the Nigerian situation with the "burning bush" that Moses saw in the wilderness, and you would not be far from the truth. The bush was on fire, yet it was not burnt. Would anyone consider that to be ordinary?

Even Moses who had seen so much in his lifetime recognized that there was something special and, in fact, supernatural about that bush. He had to draw closer to take a better look at it. Shouldn't we be doing same with Nigeria? Shouldn't we be wondering why many other nations, with fewer ethnic diversities and lesser manifestations of turbulence have broken up permanently, while Nigeria remains apparently indivisible?

But if you are still not able to get the comparison, then let me reveal yet another feature of this nation that many observers consider perhaps the most astonishing. Despite the miscellany of socio-economic maladies, misfortunes and mismanagements that have plagued Nigeria for several years, the country remains ever so prosperous and its people ever so vibrant. The enthusiasm and optimism of the average Nigerian is unparalleled. Even among the ones bent by the weight of deprivation and the ones disillusioned by the penchant for corruption among the ruling class, the aura of undying resilience and hope never stops overflowing around them.

This unique characteristic was scientifically confirmed to be true in 2010, when Nigeria was rated in a Gallup global poll as having the "happiest people on earth". The poll of 64,000 people from 53 countries around the world found Nigerians to be the most optimistic in the world.

I once read a captivating article on Nigeria and the Gallup poll which was published in the January 4, 2011 edition of the UK *Guardian*. Written by Bim Adewunmi, a freelance journalist and blogger, the article captures the extraordinary magnetism of the Nigerian spirit:

"The arrivals hall at Murtala Moammed international airport in Lagos has the kind of humidity that feels like a warm towel. The minute you shake that off, you notice the massive board that proudly welcomes you to Nigeria. Underneath the greeting, written in cheery, cursive script, is the tagline: "The happiest place in the world!"

When I last visited Nigeria, that poster made me laugh like a drain. But now a global survey has confirmed it: in a 53-country Gallup poll, Nigerians were rated at 70 points for optimism. By contrast, Britain scored a deeply pessimistic -44. Why so glum, Britain? And what in the world makes Nigerians so happy?

At first glance it's hard to see: Nigeria is seen as place where corruption thrives. The newspapers are filled with sensational allegations of crooked officials, and mind-boggling hauls ...Sectarian violence is steadily on the up, most recently with the Christmas Eve bombs in the northern city of Jos. Nor are Nigerians strangers to civil war and unrest, the most terrible being the three-year Biafran war. Then there is the grinding poverty.

To cap it all there are the advance-fee "419" scams (named for a clause in the Nigerian criminal code) – all those "princes" seeking to clear their millions in your bank account – who have embarrassingly become one of Nigeria's most famous exports.

But look harder and the optimism seems less misplaced...I'm British by birth, but got dual nationality in 2009, having lived with my Nigerian parents in the country for a large chunk of the 1990s. I had a comfortable life, and could avoid the abject poverty, crime, social inequality and the legacy of political instability. It seems natural to conclude that all these factors would put a damper on Nigerian cheerfulness. Instead, the optimism is an almost tangible thing, the joie de vivre obvious.

Daily life is hardly one glorious Technicolor dance sequence, but I have never lived in such a happy place – and I once lived in hippyville California. I can't give a definite answer, but I think the joy comes from seeing and living through the worst that life can offer; it is an optimism born of hope. Nigeria is a nation of Del Boy Trotters ("this time next year, we'll be millionaires!") – while the rest of the world believes they've got a book in them, most Nigerians believe they've got a million quid in them, too.

There's a spirit of entrepreneurship – people seem bewildered if you admit a lack of ambition. Nigerians want to go places and believe – rightly or wrongly – that they can. That drive and ambition fuels their optimism; they're working towards happiness, so they're happy..."3

What is it that gladdens and inspires this nation that seems to perpetually walk through the valleys of the shadows of death without dying? What is it that makes Nigeria to be "suffering and smiling" at the same time? What is it that heals it of its repeated wounds and makes it emerge better and stronger for it? What is it that assures and galvanizes this nation to continue to believe in itself despite internal chasms and external scoffing?

The answer lies in this question – who alone can give unshakeable joy in the midst of the most devastating crises of life? Who alone can give joy that passes all understanding – joy that is neither derived from external circumstances and perceptions nor diminished by them?

Let me say it without mincing words: God is indeed interested in the affairs of this nation. And the reason lies in His mandate for it. Undoubtedly, Nigeria has a calling that no other nation has. Let's unravel it with our keys!

TRACING THE ROOTS OF NIGERIA

How did Nigeria emerge and what were the intents of the founding founders? First, we must establish the fact that though Nigeria became a self-governing nation in 1960, following its Independence from Britain, its origin as a nation is best traced to 1914. It was in that year that Sir Frederick Lugard over saw the amalgamation of two existing British colonial states, the Protectorate of Northern Nigeria and the Colony and Protectorate of Southern Nigeria to form a single colonial entity called Nigeria. However, the name *Nigeria* itself had been suggested in 1897 by Flora Shaw, who would later become wife of Frederick Lugard.

Before 1906, the entire Nigerian territory was administered as three separate units, comprising the Lagos Protectorate, the Southern Protectorate and the Northern Protectorate. In 1906, the Protectorate of Southern Nigeria was merged with the Lagos Protectorate and officially renamed the Colony and Protectorate of Southern Nigeria. In 1914, Southern Nigeria was joined with Northern Nigeria Protectorate to form the single colony of Nigeria.

What was the motive for this audacious move by the British government? Historians who have studied the circumstances and documents relating to the amalgamation have attributed it to administrative and economic reasons. Lugard's intention was to provide a symbiotic synergy, which would ensure that both protectorates complemented each other's administrative and economic strengths. Of course, this viewpoint has been severally attacked by those who believe that the British were not actually working towards the interest of Nigeria, but in the overall interest of the British Empire.

Let me emphasize this here: Whatever it was that led to the formation of the present-day Nigeria, in January 1914, was preordained for a purpose – and the evidence is clearly seen in the numerous progresses and advancements that the country has recorded within the past 100 years of its existence.

There is another point that must be reiterated. Lord Lugard and the British government might have had "selfish reasons" for the historic amalgamation that birthed; but as we have observed from the beginning of our exploration of national greatness, God sometimes uses humans to achieve His ultimate purpose – while they are busy trying to fulfill their own parochial ambitions. Here is the truth: what makes Nigeria great, noticeable and formidable is the beauty of its diversity. In other, words, like the biblical Samson whose awesome strength lay in the intactness of his lock of hair, Nigeria's strength lies in the perpetuity of its unity. Those who are clamoring for the nation's breakup today, would discover, were God to allow it, that they had shot themselves in the foot. They would discover, too late, that the glory had departed and their strength was gone.

One truth that most historians, especially those opposed to the amalgamation, are ignorant of, or choose to neglect, is that if the Northern and Southern Protectorates had remained separate, each might have remained under the rule of the British government for much longer than 1960. In other words, it was the amalgamation that brought the needed strength and courage to break the yoke of colonialism and become a sovereign nation. In their 2014 publication in the International Journal of History and Philosophical Research, Ubaku Chika and other researchers from the Nnamdi Azikiwe University, Awka, Nigeria, stated thus:

"This development [amalgamation] changed the face of nationalist struggle as the educated elites and the traditional rulers started sharing a common historical consciousness. They began to share a vision of one Nigeria of their dream. Nationalist struggle during this period started cutting across ethnic, linguistics, and cultural boundaries. It started by acquiring the feature for justice, equality, and participation in government, and subsequently, it was

directed towards actualizing independence for the country."4

In reality, the conflicts and crises that often arise between the Northern and Southern regions of Nigeria do not occur because of the amalgamation in itself but because of some people's attempts to undo it – whether in principle or in practice. The first part of Nigeria's ultimate mandate from God therefore is to demonstrate to the world the transcending beauty of diversity. As we have noted in the creation of nations, God Himself birthed and promotes the concept of diversity in creation – because diversity reflects His greatness, wisdom, majesty and creative power.

Let's proceed with our exploration of Nigeria's roots.

THE ROAD TO INDEPENDENCE

Why did Nigeria seek independence from Britain, and with what spirit did the founding fathers fight to obtain this freedom? I will take time to provide the answer to this question. But let me begin by making a point which I would be making reference to in the later part of this chapter: The founding fathers who clamored for and rouse other Nigerians to fight for independence comprised two major groups: those who had obtained formal education in Britain, and those who had fought alongside the British army in the Second World War. Now, what was peculiar about the two groups? Acquisition of knowledge – for self-awareness and emancipation!

Nigeria's agitation for self-rule began during the 1920s, with the likes of Herbert Macauley spearheading nationalist movements. Like the biblical Moses, Macauley who had qualified as a land surveyor and civil engineer in 1893, was incensed by what he perceived to be unjust treatment of Nigerians by the colonial masters. Thus he began to lead protests in Lagos over water rates, land issues, and mishandling of the railway finances. He aroused political awareness through his newspaper, the Lagos Daily News, while leading the Nigerian National Democratic Party (NNDP).

As time went on, other individuals, groups and political organizations began to emerge, all of which contributed to the actualization of Nigeria's independence. They continuously served as vehicles that aired the grievances, expressions, and the aspirations of Nigerians. They contributed in creating political consciousness among Nigerians. Some of them had newspapers, which served them. These newspapers played significant roles in sensitizing the general public on the situation of the country. They also made public the views of the members of their organizations.

During World War II, three battalions of the Nigeria Regiment fought in the Ethiopian campaign. Nigerian units also contributed to two divisions serving with British forces in Palestine, Morocco, Sicily, and Burma, where they won many honors. Wartime experiences provided a new frame of reference for many soldiers, who interacted across ethnic boundaries in ways that were unusual in Nigeria. Most of these soldiers returned with new skills which they were eager to put to use. Besides, the soldiers had witnessed that the whites were not superior to Africans, following the defeat of the British by the Japanese in the Far East. Furthermore, in India, these soldiers came in contact with Indian strong nationalistic feeling. They saw people, who were like them, about to be granted their independence. There was also Ceylon (Sri Lanka)'s nationalist progress to inspire them. These factors prepared the minds of the returning soldiers for nationalistic reforms in their country.

As has been noted, all the individuals and groups who contributed to the Independence of Nigeria as a nation came from different ethnic, social and economic backgrounds. But that never deterred them because they knew that in the harmony of their diversity and plurality lay their power to conquer.

I asked a question at the beginning of this section: With what spirit did the founding fathers fight and win the war against colonial domination? Let historians furnish us with the answer.

On October 3, 2014, Etaghene Edirin wrote in the *New Telegraph* newspaper:

"The founding fathers in their efforts to ensure a free united country under one law made a lot of sacrifices by sidelining their comfort, tribal and religious identity to ensure that Nigeria was free.

They had dared to dream of a nation, united and strong being the pride of every black man the world over, where justice, equality and dignity of men was guaranteed, and the resources of the land were used for the benefit of the people, and development of the society."

That was the spirit – unity in courage, in overthrow of oppression, in pursuit of self-actualization, in becoming a pride to the world. The founding fathers were committed leaders, dedicated to nation building and the general development of Nigeria. Their aspiration was putting aside petty selfish and tribal interests and building a nation that would be the pride of Africa and a model to the world. Is this still the focus of present-day Nigerians?

REVISITING THE NATIONAL SYMBOLS OF NIGERIA

Having traced the roots of Nigeria and discovered vital messages from the foundations of the nation, let's confirm and consolidate such messages with the ones embedded in the symbols that constitute the unique identity of the nation.

Nigeria has the following national symbols:
- The national flag
- The coat of arms
- The national anthem
- The national pledge
- The national flower
- The national motto

Let me quickly examine the first three.

1. The Nigerian National Flag

The Nigerian national flag was designed by Pa Taiwo Akinkunmi in 1959. His was one of the over 2000 entries received by the panel of judges. After a minor adjustment, the judges adjudged his entry as the best and was adopted as the country's national flag. It was publicly hoisted for the first time on October 1, 1960, during the country's Independence celebration.

The flag is a vertical bicolor of green and white. A green band is on each side of the flag, while a white band is in the middle. Though simple, the flag is deeply meaningful. The two green bands represent Nigeria's abundant natural wealth, its vast forest and lush vegetation. The white band represents peace, unity and serenity.

The message in the flag cannot be more lucid and apt. Nigeria is abundantly blessed with fertile land and flourishing vegetation. This means that, under normal circumstances, NO NIGERIAN SHOULD GO HUNGRY. There should be more than enough agricultural products to eat, to sell and to export. Essentially, the founding fathers are telling Nigerians, through the flag, that Nigeria's primary source of prosperity is meant to be AGRICULTURE. Any other thing could come in, including petroleum, which, sadly, has become the country's obsession and bane; but such addition must be considered supplementary.

Beyond that is the need to make peace a focal pursuit, a binding factor that will ensure the sustenance and maximization of the agricultural resources that have been profusely provided by God.

Thank God for the founding fathers and the symbols with which they convey and preserve their aspirations to future generations. I'm certain that if the flag were to be redesigned in contemporary times, the color of crude oil would have been in place of the green bands; while the white would have been tinted with red - a grim reflection of the violence that has, over the years, marred the founding fathers' dream of peaceful coexistence among the citizens.

I must also emphasize that it is in the interest of Nigerians that quality attention is paid to the messages in the flag, as well as those of other symbols of the nation because power in them transcends the human agents used to express them. Here's what Pa Akinkunmi who designed the national flag said about the inspiration for the symbol:

"When you are talking about inspiration, I can tell you that God is the greatest inspirator…One couldn't have expected a science student to be able to come up with such design that has become a national symbol. I was a science student who was involved in technical drawing of equipment."5

2. The Coat of Arms

The Nigerian coat of arms features an eagle mounted on a black shield, which is trisected by two wavy bands. Two white horses support the shield, and at its base is a wreath of costus spectabilis flowers created in the national colors of white and green.

The black shield represents the fertile soil of the Nigerian nation. Like the green color of the national flag, it shows Nigeria to be richly blessed with abundant resources of the soil. Indeed, there is infinite potential in the Nigerian soil for the diligent!

The 'Y' shaped silvery bands represents the Niger and Benue Rivers, which come from different sources but join at a certain point to form the main inland waterways in Nigeria. How meaningful is this to the composition of the Nigerian populace! Nigerians may come from different roots but they are destined to be one nation. Nigerians may come from different roots but they have qualities and characteristics that bind them together into one formidable entity.

The eagle in the symbol stands for the strength of Nigerians, while the two horses facing each other symbolize dignity and pride of Nigeria. The founding fathers never envisaged Nigeria to be a weakly nation, languishing helplessly under the barrage of attacks from extremists. Neither did they foresee Nigeria as a beggarly nation, depending on foreign aid loans, and donations to survive, begging for military support and intelligence from external powers to fight internal troubles, depending on massive importation for virtually everything, including mere tooth-pick!

The Costus spectabilis is Nigeria's national flower. This colorful flower was chosen for inclusion in the coat of arms as it is found all over Nigeria and also stands for the beauty of the nation. Nigeria was envisioned to be a beautiful and attractive nation, devoid of the unpleasantness, crime and filth, with which many of our cities have become known. I say it again: Let Nigerians think!

3. The National Anthem

The Nigerian anthem, "Arise, O Compatriots," is perhaps the most popular of all the national symbols of Nigeria. It was adopted on October 1, 1978, as a replacement for the previous one, "Nigeria, We Hail Thee", which was written by Lillian Jean Williams, a British expatriate who lived in Nigeria when it achieved independence. The words of the new anthem were put to music by the Nigerian Police Band under the directorship of Benedict E. Odiase. Here is the anthem:

Arise, O compatriots,
Nigeria's call obey
To serve our Fatherland
With love and strength and faith.
The labour of our heroes past
Shall never be in vain,

To serve with heart and might
One nation bound in freedom, peace and unity.

O God of all creation
Direct our noble cause
Guide our leaders right
Help our youth the truth to know
In love and honesty to grow
And living just and true
Great lofty heights attain
To build a nation where peace
And justice shall reign.

Following in the direction of the injunction we got from Deuteronomy 32:7-8, a careful study and analysis of the above mentioned document could help us to identify the purposes, callings and the mission statement of Nigeria. For illustration sake, I would like to break down a stanza of the National Anthem here so that you can see the values, visions, directions, purposes and callings that can be deduced from this document.

- ARISE, O COMPATRIOTS

Here, the Father in heaven and our forefathers are calling us to action. To arise! This gives us a clear understanding on why we Nigerians are the way we are. Arise o compatriots is at the very foundation of who Nigerians are. We are always on the move. A proactive people, always on the rise. Unlike many other nations, even in the continent of Africa, we cannot be a passive or a laid back people. It has been planted in the very foundation of our nation to always be a people on the move. No wonder Nigerians are known to be a resilient, militant and aggressive people.

97

- NIGERIA'S CALL OBEY

This phrase is also affirming the fact that Nigerians are a people who are always arising to do something. In this case, they are arising to a call. Nigerians either home or abroad are a responsive people. Hardly would you find a group of people that would be more responsive to challenges like Nigerians are. There is this unmistakable 'CAN DO' spirit about Nigerians. Some other nations would have to use and waste a lot of resources to make their people arise or do whatsoever; but not so with Nigerians. We are a responsive people automatically. Our mentality is rising up to the occasion and challenges because it has been engraved in our National Anthem that we are a people that arise in obedience to our nation's call.

- TO SERVE OUR FATHER LAND, WITH LOVE AND STRENGTH AND FAITH

Before the Babangida/Abacha dictatorship, Nigerians were not widely seen scattered across the nations of the earth, trying to survive as we see today. As a matter of fact, different Nigerian tribal proverbs state values like "no matter how pleasant it is overseas, it is always best at home." Also, "No matter how much wealth you make abroad, you should always bring it back home."

Nigerians are a people more committed to fatherland than any other place. The usual home-coming passion during Christmas season is a very glaring proof of this. It is a time when luxury buses and planes take millions of Nigerians back to their hometowns for the end-of-year celebration. It is implanted in us to commit our love, strength and faith to our father land.

Having lived in Europe for close to 30 years myself, I know that the millions of Nigerians overseas would be ready to come back home in droves as long as they have assurances of good security, infrastructures and other basic provisions. As good as life might be treating them in other nations of the earth, the love, strength and faith of Nigerians go first to where they belong before other places.

- ## THE LABOR OF OUR HEROES PAST, SHALL NEVER BE IN VAIN

This might explain why there is a strong attachment between Nigerians and their ancestors. Even though Christianity has successfully discouraged and eradicated the worship of ancestral spirits (Thank God!). Yet, to a large expect there is overall honor and respect for the sacrifices of parents, grandparents and all those who have gone before.

Nigerians are very considerate and forgiving people. It is not in too many countries where military dictators who are former Heads of States are still honored despite wreaking so much havoc on their nations. We must take this as our national pride, our advantage not our failure. It's a wonderful spirit of forgiveness that is envied in other nations. In some other nations some of these old dictators and their families cannot even go back anymore to the nations they once ruled and ruined.

- ## TO SERVE WITH HEART AND MIGHT

Anybody who has visited Nigeria from other countries is normally always shocked at the sight of young men and women moving in-between cars and transportation to sell and hawk their goods. The zeal, energy and passion of Nigerians to survive and eke out a living for themselves always bring foreigners to a state of shock. Service, business, enterprise, zeal, energy, is the second nature of Nigerians. No wonder Nigerians are always proven to be the best in whatever nations they find themselves, in whatever endeavor of life.

- ## ONE NATION BOUND IN FREEDOM, PEACE AND UNITY

As already noted in the introduction to this chapter, Nigeria has severally defied the predictions of some of the best experts in the world as to the survival of our nation. Not too many people would believe that Nigeria would still be together today after all the struggles and challenges the country has faced. Surprisingly to everyone, the bond of unity, peace and freedom has proved stronger than the predictions of the doomsayers.

From this my short analysis above, I am sure most Nigerians would identify with the visions of the founding father. What I wish to point out though is that these truths which might be at the very fabric of our nation should not be taken for granted. They must be intentionally cultivated and purposefully pursued by the leaders and rulers of our nation so that the nation and the people will have a sense of direction and belonging.

RETURNING TO GOD AND THE SCRIPTURE

There is no denying the fact that Nigeria has the potential to be far greater than it currently is; yet there seems to be some roadblocks preventing the country from reaching the zenith of its apportioned greatness as the leader of the black nations of the world. Despite its abundant resources and the lofty goals of the founding fathers, Nigeria is still beset by grinding poverty, corruption, insecurity, poor infrastructure and high crime rate, to name a few. Some of these challenges seem intractable, as various efforts by the government, individuals and groups have proved abortive. It is wisdom then that we seek the face of God and search the Scripture for illumination.

In doing this, I will provide a background. Over the years, I have observed a major challenge with Africans generally, which I'm not surprised is also a major challenge of Nigeria, since it harbors the largest number of black people in the world. That challenge is the challenge of IGNORANCE. I may sound a bit too hard, but my focus here is not to criticize or denigrate, but to provide a candid picture of the Nigerian situation with the goal of comparing such picture with the view of the Scripture and drawing a spiritual message from it.

Now, you may prefer an alternative description of the analysis I'm about to make (if you don't think the challenge is ignorance), but for now, let me proceed to explain why I think ignorance is a major issue for Nigerians and Africans and what I think God is asking us to do about it. Since this section is on the scriptural viewpoint, I'll begin from there.

As I pointed out in the first part of this book, the Scripture asserts that all the nations of the earth descended from the three children of Noah – Shem, Ham and Japheth. Theologians and Bible scholars generally agree that Africans and, indeed, the entire black race descended from Ham, who was the youngest of the three children. Now we are told in Genesis 9:20-27 that Ham saw his father's nakedness and, apparently not knowing the right thing to do, went to tell his brothers, who were more sensible enough to cover their father, without seeing his nakedness. When Noah awoke, he was enraged at Ham's action and pronounced a curse on Canaan, his fourth son. On the other hand, Ham's brothers, Shem and Japheth, were abundantly blessed by their father.

While I wouldn't want to go into detailed theological expositions on the incident, I would like to make an inference that applies to Nigerians. Ham had every opportunity to receive the blessing that eventually went to his brothers but ignorance of the right thing to do (which some would call foolishness) made him lose out, while his brothers got the best of the situation. I will be citing more relevant references, but I want to you to begin to draw a parallel with the abundant privileges that Nigeria has to become one of the richest and grandest countries in the world.

Now, let's move on to Canaan who was actually cursed. It may interest you to know that despite the curse that was placed on Canaan and his descendants, they still actually had every opportunity to be great. God blessed their territories with an overflow of resources. In fact, in the Scripture and till today, the land of Canaan is often described as "a land flowing with milk and honey" If these people were actually cursed, why were their territories so blessed? It was obviously to make them understand the mercy of God and dedicate themselves to Him (Romans 2:4). But what did we find? IGNORANCE. Rather than acknowledging God's goodness, they devoted themselves to idolatry and other ungodly practices – till the Israelites came to subdue and supplant them!

The bottom-line is that what made the first set of people in bloodline of Nigerians to become relegated rather than celebrated was ignorance of what to do with their opportunities, blessings and privileges. Is this in any way different from what we see in Nigeria today? And as I've said, I'm using Nigeria as a suitable sample for other African and black nations of the world.

Nigeria is lavishly blessed with fertile land, overflowing resources, an energetic population and unlimited vegetation. Yet, 57 years after independence, the country is still rated as one of the top countries with the highest rate of poverty in the world. In fact, as at 2014, the World Bank rated Nigeria as one of the countries where two-thirds of the world's extreme poor are concentrated. That aside, in other aspects of national life which include health, education, scientific and technological development, spread of social and infrastructural facilities, transparency in governance, as well as general peace and stability, the country continue continues to lag behind rather than setting the pace.

What is the problem? It's simply ignorance of what to do with abundance. Let me break this down:

1. **There is ignorance about what to do with abundant natural resources.** When mass exploration and production of crude oil began in Nigeria the 1970s, agriculture, which placed the country among the best economies in the world, was abandoned. The popular groundnut pyramid of Kano, the palm oil and rubber plantations of the east and the cocoa plantations of the west began to die away. Importation replaced exportation. Money was flowing in from oil, but the national currency was crumbling and the majority of the populace was starving. The situation continues till now.

2. **Ignorance of what to do with abundant human resource.** Majority of Nigerians are intelligent, creative, energetic and ambitious. If this resource alone is sufficiently recognized and harnessed, the country would have advanced tremendously. But what do we find? Because many of the best brains in science, medicine, sports, arts and so on, are not often recognized or appreciated, foreign countries lure them away with juicy offers – resulting in what has come to be known as "brain drain".

3. **Ignorance of what to do with skills and opportunities.** Lots of Nigerian youth have special skills and entrepreneurial abilities with which they could do great things for themselves and their country. But what do we find? Talents and skills are either wasted away in perpetual complaints about "unfavorable environment" or diverted into dubious ventures, such as the globally infamous "yahoo-yahoo" or "419 scam".

4. **Ignorance of what to do with money.** There are people who have access to money – whether public money or

through personal accumulation. So much could be done with such money to invest in the country, start businesses or build manufacturing firms. Instead, we are daily inundated with stories of public officials looting billions of money and stashing such in foreign accounts – thereby helping other countries to boost their economies while the local economy and population continue to suffer. Also, there are private individuals who simply view access to money as an opportunity to depend on imported products and living flamboyantly.

5. **Ignorance of what to do with diversity.** The diversity of the Nigerian population has continued to be used by many in the country as a basis for dragging the nation downward and backward, rather than lifting it upward and forward. Ignorance makes them only see the problem, instead of potentials of the country's diversity. So much time and energy is wasted on agitation for breakup, instead of focusing on and maximizing the benefits of diversity. Interestingly, many other countries not suffering from such ignorance continue to encourage and reap the fruits of the diversity of their cultures. Some go as far as operating Open Immigration policy, to encourage people from other places to come in and contribute their quota to the development of their countries. This way, they keep getting the best of brains and manpower who are helping to advance their countries. As former U.S. Secretary of State, Colin Powell, once said, "America is a nation of nations, made up of people from every land, of every race and practicing every faith. Our diversity is not a source of weakness; it is a source of strength, it is a source of our success."

6. **Ignorance of the power of righteousness, integrity and accountability.** There is pervasive ignorance of the fact that working towards collective interest, instead of personal interest, works for the overall good of everyone. Whether in public, civil or private service, most people in present-day Nigeria often scramble to get whatever they can get for themselves, even at the expense of others. This is the cause of the massive corruption that pervades virtually every aspect of our national life.

I have other points I could give but since this is not my major focus here, let me simply summarize the challenge with Nigeria in the words of Jeff Okoroafor, who wrote in 2013 thus:

"The root cause of our national challenge is not in our over exaggerated religious, tribal and ethnic affections but our selfishness and absolute lack of principles. There is a fundamental problem when we allow our parochial considerations assume and command our allegiances over our national consciousness. Whatever gives us undue advantage over others will never establish our collective faith, trust and hope. Our challenge is the penchant for undue reward and benefit of opportunism, mediocrity and nepotism. The resultant delusion is everyone seeking for a "one Nigeria" yet hardly is anyone willing to give up his or her allegiance and commitment to his or her religion, tribe, ethnicity and socio-cultural affiliations. We all desire a progressive nation yet nobody is prepared to give up the destructive and unjust reward of nepotism and sectionalism for merit, honor and hard work. This is Nigeria's dilemma."

So, what is God's calling upon this nation which has so much potential to be a SUPERPOWER? In answering this, I'll still refer to the Scripture by citing examples of two Africans who knew what Nigerians and Africans really need to be doing.

The first example is the Queen of Sheba, who, despite all her riches and her high position went in search of knowledge and wisdom from King Solomon (1 Kings 10:1-13).

The second example is the Ethiopian Eunuch, who, despite his high status and obvious privilege in the palace of Queen Candace, admitted to Philip that he needed knowledge and understanding (Acts 8:26-40).

From these people, I'll draw three messages for Nigeria.

Nigeria needs to get developmental knowledge and ideas (and not endless financial and material donations) from other countries on how to turn its abundant resources to its maximum advantage. Getting such knowledge could involve travelling to such countries to observe and learn like the Queen of Sheba and the Ethiopian Eunuch. Besides, both the leaders and the citizens need to learn what it takes to turn their nation to the pride of the world. Queen Sheba was a leader, while the Ethiopian Eunuch was serving under someone.

From our two examples, neither the Queen nor the Eunuch stayed back in the places where they got knowledge; and neither of them expected their mentors to spoon-feed them for life. Let Nigerians who have gained knowledge and experienced better living conditions in foreign countries not focus on "enjoying themselves" in these countries for life. All they have seen and learnt must be put into practical use in their own country.

Let there be practical applications of principles of national development by all. Queen Sheba returned to her homeland with all she had learnt which would be applied in her capacity as a LEADER. The Ethiopian Eunuch also returned with all he had heard, which would be applied in his capacity as an officer under a leader. Let every Nigerian know that the task of nation building cannot be left to the leader or the citizens alone. Everyone has to learn what it takes to build a prosperous nation. Everyone has to play his or her role in the actual process of nation building. Everyone has to adapt and apply what has been learnt or observed with the national environment.

FURTHER APPLICATIONS

Let me add that for Nigeria to attain her potential, the values and virtues enshrined in the national symbols and documents must be rigorously propagated and promoted both by the government of the day and also by conscious citizens.

We must interweave all these values and virtues into every aspect of our national life. Schools, from kindergarten and nursery to tertiary institutions, must adopt these principles and values in their curricular and educational programs.

Since we are living in the 21st century that is mostly influenced by the media and entertainers, the government and other individual non-governmental organizations must launch comprehensive programs to use entertainment and media to spread these virtues and values. The Nigerian Nollywood and music industry must not just be allowed to propagate witchcraft and other vices any longer. Instead, the practitioners must begin to find a way to include these values in their scripts and lyrics.

If these principles, values and virtues (outlined below) could be integrated into the country's educational system, music and movie industry etc, we will in no time be able to change the national psyche of the Nigerian nation. Every Nigerian must take up the challenge of aggressively propagating the values and virtues that are supposed to be the core of who we are.

The great Professor Dora Akunyili attempted to bring about this vision when she launched the "Nigeria: Good People, Great Nation" campaign. That campaign has since died off because it was only a government initiated program. Except a different approach is adopted, the same fate awaits the "Change Begins with

Me" reorientation program recently launched by President Buhari.

Every Nigerian must know that to avoid this type of stillborn ideas, we all must own this movement of regeneration of values in our people. Right now, Nigerians are better known for their vices instead of their values. Almost nobody knows the list I am about to provide below as part of our national heritage. This list must be adopted by every Nigerian. The listed virtues must be promoted by every religious and secular institution. Every business organization and government parastatal must make it a duty to propagate these values and virtues at any given opportunity.

It is not enough just to sing the national anthem and recite the national pledge, the following values and virtues must become part of the moral fabric of every Nigerian.

The list of our national values, virtues and missions include:

Action

Brotherhood

Resilience

Obedience

Patriotism

Service

Love

Strength

Faith

Honor

Freedom

Peace

Unity

Truth

Justice

Development

Progress

Diligence

Militancy

Pro-activeness

The good thing about these values is that they transcend tribal and religious allegiances. They are values that are universal. So, churches and mosques must teach these values. School assemblies and university lecture halls must all adopt these tenets, such that nobody finishes any school without having these virtues as part of their character and behavior.

This is how nations become great!

Nations and peoples are great, not by the virtue of their wealth but by the wealth of their virtues. If our nation Nigeria will ever be great, we must be great in our virtues. As already highlighted above, we have the virtues, but we neither know nor imbibe them in our character and we don't live by them. This is the challenge we must solve.

It is true that we have to harness a great deal of our wealth of natural resources; but I am sure that we have also painfully realized that natural resources don't make a nation great, only great virtues do. If we could inculcate the highlighted virtues into every single Nigerian, we will be remembered in the comity of nations as a great people and a great nation.

CHAPTER SIX

FRANCE: THE SPECTACULAR THINKER WITH A PECULIAR STINKER

The French nation has always been a source of wonder and fascination to the world, for different reasons. From year to year, multitudes of people throng it in order to savor their share of its famed attractions. Recently, the United Nations World Tourism Organization noted that in 2014 alone, the country recorded 83.7 million visitors. Only one other nation came close - the United States - which recorded 74.8 million visits, despite being more than four times the size of France. Records for other years show a similar trend, making the nation arguably the most visited in the world in recent times.

Diverse reasons have been adduced for the world's fascination with France – its rich culture and military might; its capital, Paris, being "the most romantic destination" in the world; its couture fashion houses; its classical art museums and monuments; its medieval and port cities; its tranquil villages and inviting climates;

its mountain ranges and different coastlines; and, of course, it's sophisticated cuisine, comprising a very wide spectrum of food, wines and beers. It did not come as a surprise for many, when in 2010, France became the first nation to have its cuisine recognized by UNESCO as "intangible cultural heritage", reinforcing the widespread admiration for its gastronomy.

However, no other quality has distinguished France as a spectacular and significant nation of the world as its INTELLECTUAL PROWESS. Until recent years, what had always placed this nation on a pedestal of greatness and marked it out as one on the path of a preordained destiny is its depth of thought. In his widely acclaimed book, *"How the French Think: An Affectionate Portrait of an Intellectual People"*, internationally-renowned historian, Sudhir Hazareesingh, asks, "Why are the French such an exceptional nation? Why do they think they are so exceptional?" and then goes ahead to provide this poignant answer: "The French take pride in the fact that their history and culture have decisively shaped the values and ideals of the modern world. French ideas are no less distinct in their form: while French thought is abstract, stylish and often opaque, it has always been bold and creative, and driven by the relentless pursuit of innovation."[1]

While Greece is often said to be the cradle of ancient philosophy, France could be described as the powerhouse of modern philosophy. Perhaps more than any other nation of the world, this country, in the past few centuries, has produced more notable thinkers and writers, whose depths of thought and philosophies not only shaped the course of events in the nation itself (including the French Revolution) but actually triggered transformations in many socio-political systems of the world.

From Peter Abelard, whom the *Chambers Biographical Dictionary* describes as "the keenest thinker and boldest theologian of the 12th Century" to René Descartes, Voltaire (François-Marie Arouet), Jean-Jacques Rousseau, Denis Diderot, Auguste Comte,

Simone de Beauvoir, Jean-Paul Sartre, Albert Camus, Victor Hugo, Michel Foucault and René Cassin, French philosophers and writers expressed ground-breaking ideas that reverberated across the globe and the effects were phenomenal.

As the UK Guardian of June 13, 2015 rightly noted:

"An enduring source of the French pride is that their ideas and historical experiences have decisively shaped the values of other nations…Through the revolutionary epics of the late 18th and early 19th centuries, French civilian and military heroes inspired national liberators throughout the world, from Wolfe Tone in Ireland and Toussaint L'Ouverture in Haiti to Simón Bolívar in Latin America. The Napoleonic Civil Code was widely adopted by newly independent states during the 19th century, and the emperor's art of war was celebrated by progressive writers and poets across Europe, from William Hazlitt to Adam Mickiewicz, but also by Japanese samurai warriors and Tartar tribesmen (a Central Asian folk song celebrated "Genghis Khan and his nephew Napoleon"), and by the Vietnamese revolutionary hero Võ Nguyên Giáp."2

This observation is, indeed, striking and worth pondering upon. There is no denying that the most powerful catalyst of progress, civilization and advancement in all spheres of human life is thought. All inventions are products of robust imaginations. In fact, writing shortly after the Second World War, French historian, André Siegfried, minced no words when he declared that French thought had been the driving force behind all the major advances of human civilization. Logically, therefore, it is expected that France should be blazing the trail of excellence in its affairs, as well as dominance in world affairs. France, which has a much longer history than countries like USA, China and Russia, should be leading these countries in all aspects.

But, in reality, how much have the French people leveraged their uncommon ability to think to their advantage in setting the pace of progress in their nation and influencing other nations for good? Or let's be more realistic - as many concerned observers of the French nation have been doing lately – and pose a more direct question: IS THE FRENCH NATION STILL THINKING AT ALL? Does it still retain its innovative thinking ability? If not, why not?

Johnathan Fenby, in his book, *The History of Modern France*, states unequivocally that "while justly proud of the nation's achievements since the Revolution, the French have become prisoners of the heritage of their past" – an indirect way of saying that the nation had long neglected its "magic wand" for unparalleled greatness.

But if we are to assume that France still wears its thinking cap, then the question is, what is the preoccupation of its thoughts these days? And, most importantly, what really should the French be doing to maximize their mental potentialities for the fulfillment of their distinct purpose as a nation? The answer will be unveiled as we explore the roots of the nation and the vision of its founding fathers.

TRACING THE ROOTS OF THE FRENCH NATION

The evolution of the French nation as we know it today is one of the most eventful in history. In other words, several notable events, triggered by the pulsations of vibrant minds, have combined to shape the course of the nation's history for centuries. I think this is because the French always tended to be ahead of their time and peers in progressive reflections.

In looking at the roots of the French nation, therefore, I will be focusing on key historical watersheds that really helped to shape its identity, define its people and made it an exemplary spectacle for other nations to emulate. These historical milestones can be roughly divided into what I have encapsulated in the 6Rs – Royalty, Renaissance, Reformation, Revolution, Restoration and Republicanism.

1. Royalty

Even though archeological excavations indicate that the French nation had been continuously settled since Paleolithic times (i.e., earliest period of human development), historians believe that France, once called "Gaul", was settled by the Celts who migrated from the Rhine valley to the South of Gaul in 800 BC. These Celtic Gauls, according to Bible scholars, were, in fact, dispersed Israelites, most likely from the tribe of Reuben (I will be making detailed reference to this later).

Julius Caesar conquered part of Gaul in 57–52 B.C. , and it remained Roman until the Franks invaded it in the 5th century. Charlemagne, King of the Franks, who was also known as Charles the Great, played a significant role in the evolution of the French nation. He had, during the early Middle Ages, united a large part of Europe to form an empire. Until then, the various territories had been under feudal lords. Following Charlemagne's death, the Treaty of Verdun (in 843 AD) divided the territories within his empire corresponding roughly to France, Germany, and Italy among his three grandsons. Charles the Bald inherited France.

By 987, the crown had passed to Hugh Capet, and as the crown continued this way, monarchy was steadily consolidated in France, while feudalism gradually died away. This brought unprecedented development to the French people. The great monastic orders and emerging towns that came with the metamorphosis of the nation from the grip of feudal lords to the control of royalty opened the floodgates of economic and cultural advancement.

It was within this period that the brilliant capabilities of the French mind began to find expression. In fact, by 1328 and the accession of Philip VI, not only had France already boasted the highest achievements of medieval European culture - its Romanesque and Gothic architecture – but it had actually become the most powerful nation in Europe.

But that was just the beginning. Within the reign of Louis XIV (1643–1715), who brought absolute monarchy to its height, the beauty of the French royalty had reached its highpoint. The time of his reign was a period of unprecedented prosperity in which France became the dominant power in the arts and sciences. This was a time that many other nations were still struggling to find their feet intellectually. Having been a great artist himself from age seven, King Louis gave maximum backing to full expression of the vibrancy of the French mind by encouraging the flourishing of French arts and literature.

Aside being a discriminating patron of the great literary and artistic figures of France's classical age, Louis XIV's government established or developed, in rapid succession, academies for painting and sculpture (1663), inscriptions (1663), French artists at Rome (1666), and science (1666); followed by the Paris Observatory (1667) and the academies of architecture (1671) and music (1672). His most enduring legacy was Château de Versailles – which is still recognized as the embodiment of classical French art and has been on UNESCO's World Heritage List for over 30 years. This magnificent court was the center of the then Western world.

2. Renaissance

While the Royalty flourished in France, with the attendant festoonery of artistic, literary and intellectual advancements, another form of tremendous blossoming was being experienced by these people of uncommon imaginative ability. It was simply termed "Renaissance", which means "rebirth".

It was a rebirth, indeed, as the cultural history of France experienced a clean break from the Middle Ages, paving way for radical transformations that affected every aspect of the socio-cultural life of the French people – from the arts, to music to architecture. Many artistic, literary and technological developments emerged in the country within this period.

Actually, it was under François 1, king of France from 1515 to 1547, that Renaissance art and architecture first blossomed in France. Shortly after coming to the throne, François, a cultured and intelligent monarch, invited the popular artist, Leonardo da Vinci from Italy to come and work in France. Leonardo came to live at Amboise, bringing with him paintings and drawings, many of which are still in France today, notably at the Louvre, which has the world's largest collection of Leonardo's paintings, including the *Mona Lisa*, known in *France as La Joconde*.

François I not only encouraged the Renaissance style of art in France but also set about building fine Renaissance buildings in his capital city, and outside it. The most magnificent examples of early French Renaissance architecture are the royal château at Chambord, in the Loire valley, and the rebuilding of the royal palace at Fontainebleau south of Paris.

What I want you to see here however is not the avalanche of changes that the rebirth brought to the French nation but the way the rebirth itself began. What became known in history as French Renaissance was actually an adaptation of artistic and cultural ideas imported from Italy. This goes a long way to show that the French mind is not just an active mine for generating literary, intellectual and artistic ideas, but it is actually a fertile ground for germinating and multiplying same.

3. Reformation

Worthy of note is the fact that it was not only in the areas of intellectualism and literary proficiencies that the French had historically proved to be progressive; they were not lagging behind in the religious segment either. The highpoint of this was the introduction of the Protestant faith to the nation, which brought huge religious enlightenment to the people, leading to the weakening of the grip of papal powers and the dogmas of the Catholic Church on their minds.

Many people may not know this, but some five years or more before Martin Luther posted his **Theses** in Wittenburg, Germany, in 1517, another reformed monk, Jacques Lefevre (aka Faber Stapulensis) was preaching reform in Paris. Lefevre was a Carmelite monk with a reputation for having an enquiring mind. As a scholar, he travelled abroad and studied history, mathematics, philosophy and theology. He was also proficient in the ancient languages of Greek and Hebrew as well as Latin. He had a presentiment that change was necessary and being open-minded he read the Bible in search of material for a treatise on the lives of the saints. In so doing he was struck by the concept of salvation by faith alone. In 1512 he published a commentary on the Epistles of St Paul in which he declared:

"It is God who gives us, by faith, that righteousness which grace alone justifies to eternal life".

Other great and inspired minds such as John Calvin helped greatly to propagate the Protestant doctrines, leading to the conversion of many. These converts are those popularly known today as the Huguenots. And even though brutal persecutions and massacres ensued from the ruling powers who were bent on the perpetuity of the Catholic monopoly of religion, the protestant faith had been established and the impacts continue to be felt today.

4. Revolution

One thing I have observed and continue to emphasize about the foundations of the French nation is the advantaged position they were placed because of their cognitive proficiency. The cumulative effect of all that I have shown you so far is that by the end of the eighteenth century, the French nation was already brimming with all the indices of intellectual and social maturity. When a nation reaches such pinnacle and is still YEARNING to go further, it is expected that a seismic shift must occur in its status and structure. In the case of the French nation, the result was the popular revolution that overhauled its entire socio-political order.

The revolution began in 1789 and by the time it was over in 1799, the monarchical system of government had been dislodged and replaced with republicanism. Unsurprisingly, as the pace-setter that France was meant to be in reformist thinking, that revolution proved to be one of the most important events in human history. The after-effect reverberated throughout the world, triggering the global decline of absolute monarchies while replacing them with republics and liberal democracies in many other countries of the world.

Again, let us ask ourselves. What led to such massive social and political upheaval in the French nation and then to other parts of the world? The power of the radical mind of the French. According to Jean Jaure, a historian, at the time of the revolution, "French thought had become conscious of its grandeur and wanted to apply its methods of analysis and deduction to all of reality, society and nature alike. The French bourgeoisie had become conscious of its power, its wealth, its rights, and its near infinite possibilities of development. In a word, the bourgeoisie had attained class consciousness while French thought touched the consciousness of the universe. These are the two ardent resources, the two sources of the fire of the Revolution. It was through them that it was possible, and it was through them that it was great."4

Unlike what obtains in many nations of the world today (and sadly even in modern-day France itself) the founding fathers of the French nation were not such that gave room to mediocrity, complacency or substandard living. Whatever was defective in the socio-political order, they thought of a way out of it; and whatever seemed good, they thought of a better way. The monarchical system of government (royalty) certainly had its advantages, considering the numerous gains it brought to the French as I already pointed out above; but as soon as it became obvious that the royalty had outlived its usefulness, the people quickly thought of a way to dispense with it.

Issues that stirred the leaders of the revolution and indeed the entire French nation included rising social and economic inequality, new political ideas emerging from the Enlightenment, perceived economic mismanagement, unmanageable national debt, and political mismanagement on the part of the then monarch, King Louis XVI.

5. Republicanism

As I have pointed out above, one significant upshot of the French Revolution is the emergence of the French Republic, the first of which was headed by Napoleon Bonaparte. The republic was founded on September 22, 1792, following the abolition of the monarchy and the Declaration of the Rights of Man and the Citizen in 1789.

It can indeed be said that the modern history of the French nation began from this time. The period marked the concretization and institutionalization of the core values of the French nation. It was within this period that the French national anthem, *The Marseillaise*, was composed. It was then, too, that the national motto of France, *"Liberty, equality, fraternity"* was developed. Within this same period, also, France became highly centralized, with all decisions made in Paris. The political geography was completely reorganized and made uniform.

Altogether, there have been five republics in the history of France: First Republic (1792–1804); Second Republic (1848–

1852); Third Republic (1870–1940); Fourth Republic (1946–1958); French Fifth Republic (1958–Present)

6. Restoration

I told you already why I so much love the French. When in 1804, Napoleon, in a bid to consolidate his hold on power, declared himself emperor and from then on began to fully exhibit dictatorial tendencies, the French would have none of it. Interestingly, you would have thought that, having orchestrated the republican system of government that paved way for Napoleon as a national leader, the French would waste some time wallowing in regret and wondering if there was a way out having brought the entire trouble on themselves. But that's naturally abhorrent to the quintessential French mind. Having observed that the republic had been technically hijacked and derailed, they quickly reverted to the old system of government. The French had the monarchy restored and the emperor was banished.

Even though there was still going to be a return to republicanism later on, the French had made it clear what kind of people they were and the kind of nation they were building for themselves – a nation where freedom, equality, justice and progress (propelled by the power of the mind) would be permanently entrenched.

REVISITING THE NATIONAL SYMBOLS OF THE FRENCH NATION

In all of the various events that shaped its colorful history, the national values of the French nation gradually evolved and became established. All these are codified in the country's national symbols which I will be highlighting below:

1. The French National Anthem ("La Marseillaise")

Here again the matchless beauty of the French mind shines

ever so brightly. Of all the national anthems in the world, "La Marseillaise" is arguably the best known and most inspirational! In fact, many historians actually rank it the best national anthem in the world!

Someone said of the French anthem, "By far the greatest national anthem of all time. La Marseillaise is powerful, majestic, inspiring, and also has a great deal of pomp and engenders national pride and confidence." Describing it, David Walker, professor emeritus of French at the University of Sheffield, UK, said that, unlike the British national anthem, "God Save the Queen," *La Marseillaise* is not an aristocratic song. It's about the people, it's about being a citizen. It's a rousing anthem and people can sing it with gusto".5

I shall be reproducing the complete anthem here, but before then, let me briefly explain how it was birthed. I need to do this to show you what makes the anthem and its message so significant to the calling of the French people.

The song was written in 1792 by Claude Joseph Rouget de Lisle in Strasbourg, after the declaration of war by France against Austria. It was originally titled "Chant de guerre pour l'Armée du Rhin" ("War Song for the Rhine Army").

What actually happened was that as the French Revolution continued, the monarchies of Europe became concerned that revolutionary fervor would spread to their countries. So, they resolved to either stop the revolution, or at least restrict it to France. On April 25 1792, baron Philippe-Frédéric de Dietrich, the mayor of Strasbourg, got a report of imminent invasion of France by Austria. He therefore requested his guest, 31-year-old Rouget de Lisle, who was a soldier and amateur violinist, to compose a song "that will rally our soldiers from all over to defend their homeland that is under threat".

Rouget de Lisle ran back to his room from that meeting and

in the space of just a few hours wrote *La Marseillaise*. It must have been by divine inspiration because what he produced was a revolutionary song, an anthem to freedom, a patriotic call to mobilize all the citizens and an exhortation to fight against tyranny and foreign invasion.

The French National Convention adopted the song as the Republic's anthem in 1795. It acquired its nickname *La Marseillaise* after being sung in Paris by volunteers from Marseille marching on the capital. The song is the first example of the "European march" anthemic style. The anthem's evocative melody and lyrics have led to its widespread use as a song of revolution and its incorporation into many pieces of classical and popular music.

As I promised before, I will reproduce the entire translated anthem here. Even though it's the first stanza and the chorus that are often sung during ceremonies these days, it is important to have a glimpse of what the entire anthem contains so as to know why it so much reflects the ideals of the French nation.

Arise, children of the Fatherland,
The day of glory has arrived!
Against us tyranny's
Bloody banner is raised, (repeat)
Do you hear, in the countryside,
The roar of those ferocious soldiers?
They're coming right into your arms
To cut the throats of your sons, your women!

To arms, citizens,
Form your battalions,
Let's march, let's march!
Let an impure blood
Soak our fields!

What does this horde of slaves,
Of traitors and conspiratorial kings want?
For whom are these vile chains,
These long-prepared irons? (repeat)
Frenchmen, for us, ah! What outrage
What fury it must arouse!
It is us they dare plan
To return to the old slavery!

To arms, citizens...

What! Foreign coorts
Would make the law in our homes!
What! These mercenary phalanxes
Would strike down our proud warriors! (repeat)
Great God! By chained hands
Our brows would yield under the yoke
Vile despots would have themselves
The masters of our destinies!

To arms, citizens...

Tremble, tyrants and you traitors
The shame of all parties,
Tremble! Your parricidal schemes
Will finally receive their reward! (repeat)
Everyone is a soldier to combat you
If they fall, our young heroes,
The earth will produce new ones,
Ready to fight against you!

To arms, citizens...

Frenchmen, as magnanimous warriors,
Bear or hold back your blows!
Spare those sorry victims,
Who arm against us with regret. (repeat)
But not these bloodthirsty despots,
These accomplices of Bouillé,
All these tigers who, mercilessly,
Rip their mother's breast!

To arms, citizens...

Sacred love of the Fatherland,
Lead, support our avenging arms
Liberty, cherished Liberty,
Fight with thy defenders! (repeat)
Under our flags, may victory
Hurry to thy manly accents,
May thy expiring enemies,
See thy triumph and our glory!

To arms, citizens...

(Children's Verse)
We shall enter the (military) career
When our elders are no longer there,
There we shall find their dust
And the trace of their virtues (repeat)
Much less keen to survive them
Than to share their coffins,

We shall have the sublime pride
Of avenging or following them

To arms, citizens...

SOME FOOD FOR THOUGHT

Someone rightly described the French anthem as "the ultimate anthem of defiance and resistance." So, my question is: *Defiance against what?* Of course, it was defiance against external oppression, tyranny and retrogression; but beyond that, it was defiance against complacency, mediocrity, and timidity. It portrayed the French as a nation of perpetually forward-thinking people, a people that would always strive towards excellence and reject anything considered inferior or commonplace. And interestingly, the anthem itself has proved to be a living testimony of its content and intent. Various attempts had been made to subdue and invalidate it. The anthem survived two Empires, the Restoration and other major oppositions before finally being officialized by the Republic in 1946.

Here is another vital question: hundreds of years after the original words of the anthem were penned and sung, how has the French nation fared? The anthem, as I have said, is a call to conquer potentially limiting forces and embrace excellence in all spheres of life. So, what is France's position generally in comparison with other nations? Personally, I found it disturbing that of all indices whereby a nation is deemed to be exceptional – economy, environment, globalization, military, politics, social life and technological advancements - France takes no leading position in any.

The only area where France leads the world is that which I already pointed out at the beginning of this chapter – TOURISM. This, on the surface, may seem normal and indeed commendable.

But when you give it a deeper consideration, you find out that it is actually something to be worried about. Why do I say this? The answer lies in knowing what usually attracts tourists to a country. These features are called "tourist attractions". The Wikipedia describes a tourist attraction as "a place of interest where tourists visit, typically for its inherent or exhibited natural or cultural value, historical significance, natural or built beauty, offering leisure, adventure and amusement."

To put it simply, France is only popular for its past glories and achievements. People throng the country to see landmarks laid either naturally by God or physically by the founding fathers of the nation. What then are the current citizens doing? The citizens seem no longer interested in taking up intellectual arms against social, economic and political stagnancy and mediocrity. This confirms the concerns which many have long held that the French nation is no longer thinking – and when it does, it's mostly about trivialities!

2. The French National Motto

The French national motto says a lot about the vision and passion of its founding fathers: **"Liberty. Equality. Fraternity (or Brotherhood)"**. These three concepts formed the driving force behind the great revolution and the institution of the republic in France. What did the fathers mean by "liberty"? This is clearly defined in Article 4 of the 1789 Declaration of the Rights of Man and Citizen (Similar to the Americans' Declaration of Independence). According to the document, "Liberty consists of being able to do anything that does not harm others: thus, the exercise of the natural rights of every man or woman has no bounds other than those that guarantee other members of society the enjoyment of these same rights".

Similarly, the term, "equality", was coined in Article 6 of the 1789 Declaration in terms of judicial equality and merit-based entry to government. It says "[The law] must be the same for all, whether it protects or punishes. All citizens, being equal in its eyes, shall be equally eligible to all high offices, public positions and employments, according to their ability, and without other distinction than that of their virtues and talents."

Fraternity, on its part, is a word associated with the idea of community, which is a body of people that share a common interest or purpose or people working together to achieve a common goal. And, indeed, as a result of this sense of brotherhood, the founding fathers of France found it relatively easy to achieve whatever they set their minds on. Their sense of togetherness and mutual empathy was so strong that neither royalty, nor revolutionists nor emperors could stop them from collectively redressing injustice and tyranny.

It may interest you to know that the French national motto actually influenced the First Article of the 1948 Universal Declaration of Human Rights. The three keywords are represented in the document. The document says, "All human beings are born free and equal in dignity and rights. They are endowed with reason and conscience and should act towards one another in a spirit of brotherhood." This is another legacy of the French's creative contribution to the world.

3. Marianne: The Embodiment of the Values of the French

I cannot comprehensively discuss the national symbols of France, without giving special attention to this emblematic figure. If you have ever visited France or studied its history, you must have come across Marianne. She is one of the most prominent symbols of the French Republic, and is officially used on most government documents. Her profile stands out on the official government logo of the country; it is engraved on French euro coins and appears on French postage stamps; it was also featured on the former franc currency.

Marianne came into being through a decree of 1792, which stipulated that the state seal was to be changed and "should henceforth bear the figure of France in the guise of a woman dressed after the fashion of Antiquity, standing upright, her right hand holding a pikestaff surmounted by a Phrygian bonnet, or Liberty bonnet, and her left hand resting on a bundle of arms: at her feet, a tiller."

Someone says of this symbol, "Marianne is the embodiment of the French Republic. Marianne represents the permanent values that found her citizens' attachment to the Republic: "Liberty, Equality, Fraternity"."6

This is why I said she cannot be ignored in our understanding of the goals of the founding fathers of France for the nation.

Actually, the reason I'm mentioning Marianne here is not just for her historical significance but the powerful message that is intended to be conveyed by her depiction. Marianne often appears wearing a helmet and bearing arms, like Athena of Greece. What's the significance of the warrior attire and posture? It is intended to convey the message that even though Marianne is meant to portray the image of freedom, liberty and fraternity which the French people were to consistently follow after, none of these ideals would be achieved without some form of conflict.

This is the hidden message for the French: There is always a price to pay for excellence. A battle to fight to obtain freedom. There will always be oppositions in the quest to living a life of purpose. But most importantly, it will take real, consistent warfare (it doesn't have to be physical; it could be just intellectual) for a nation to stay true to the purpose of its creation and calling.

Here again, we must pause to ask. Are French citizens making much effort to stay true to the ideals of their founding fathers? Do they realize, as their anthem and other symbols portray, that preventing invasion of evil, tyranny, mediocrity and other anomalies is never achieved by a *laissez-faire* attitude to life? Do the French, despite being surrounded by these echoes of warfare, even think of the need to still fight any battle at all? And of course, when I say battle, I'm not talking of peace-keeping missions or forming alliances with other nations to combat a perceived common enemy. I'm actually talking about the internal battles that France has to fight to maintain its uniqueness and fulfill the purpose of its creation as a nation!

Again, just as the national anthem and other symbols of the French nation, attempts have been made to obliterate Marianne from the history of France; but just as an ancient landmark that cannot be removed, she continues to shine bright – passing the message to the people of France of not just its significance but the attitude that is expected of them in the face of pressure to compromise their founding values!

4. The French National Flag

The French flag dates back to the days of the French Revolution. However, in a rather thoughtful and very strategic move – typical of France's founding fathers - something of the pre-revolution era was retained in the flag.

Ordinarily the French tricolor flag, having blue (left), white (center) and red (right) bands should just have had two colors, blue and red, which had a major significance for the revolutionists. Members of the Parisian militia that stormed the Bastille on July 14, 1789, heralding the revolution, had worn blue and red cockades on their hats. However, prior to the revolution, France had traditionally been represented by a plain white flag - a sign of purity and strength. This was something the founding fathers never wanted to dispense with. They seemed to be establishing and preserving a message for the French people of all generations – that in the midst of all their potentialities, aspirations and achievements, PURITY OF CHARACTER AND PURPOSE must be at the center of their national life.

Is the French nation paying any attention to this – considering the depths of moral and spiritual decay that pervades the nation? Let's consider this in detail, as we study the biblical perspective of the calling of the French nation.

RETURNING TO GOD AND THE SCRIPTURE

As I have demonstrated in the case of the two other nations we have considered so far, my goal under this section is not to delve into extensive theological arguments and postulations. My goal is to show you connections between biblical descriptions and the present conditions of each of the nations we are examining.

So, we come to the nation of France and we wonder if there are pointers in the Scripture that relates to this nation. The answer will be provided shortly; but first, let me ask, can you recall the singular attribute that I have repeatedly emphasized and illustrated as the most distinguishing strength of the French people? Good. It is the power of their thinking faculty! Is there a particular tribe in the Scripture that was singled out for this same attribute? Certainly and very CLEARLY. Judges 5:15-16 says: **"And the princes of Issachar were with Deborah; even Issachar, and also Barak: he was sent on foot into the valley. For the divisions of Reuben there were great thoughts of heart. Why abodest thou among the sheepfolds, to hear the bleatings of the flocks? For the divisions of Reuben there were great searchings of heart."**

You have it there. And you probably will understand why, as I mentioned earlier, I tend to agree with the Bible historians who have provided a number of historical, genealogical and geographical proofs that the earliest settlers in France were actually descendants of Reuben. But we must go further than this, as there are other striking resemblances that we cannot just shove aside as mere coincidences – especially as there is a powerful message for the French nation in all this!

So, this Reuben, what more do we know about him, apart from the fact that his descendants were great thinkers? First, we must look into that same passage again before going back to the earliest history. On what occasion were the people in the passage engaging in **"great thoughts of heart"**? At a time of warfare! In other words, something positive was being mentioned about these people but in a very negative context.

Let me break this down further. These divisions of Reuben were, from all indications, a people who, despite having great potential of the mind also had the weakness of misdirecting their efforts and demonstrating lack of discipline and tact. This robbed them of the commendation and laurels they could have gotten, had they been able to make valuable contributions when needed the most.

And again, we must find out: This discrepancy of character traits, could it have been just an accidental slip on the part of the descendants or is it something that was inherent in their bloodline? Let's consider the man himself from whom they descended.

This is a declaration from Genesis 49:3-4:

"Reuben, thou art my firstborn, my might, and the beginning of my strength, the excellency of dignity, and the excellency of power: Unstable as water, thou shalt not excel; because thou wentest up to thy father's bed; then defiledst thou it: he went up to my couch".

This was Jacob, Reuben's father, foretelling the fate of Reuben and his descendants. Even from a purely logical point of view, something doesn't seem to add up here. Why would someone who represented the excellency of DIGNITY and MIGHT – in other words, full of great potentials to succeed and exceed expectations – not be able to excel, that is, take the leading position among his siblings? The answer is right there: **"Unstable as water..."** - fickle, lacking moral backbone, undisciplined.

The account to which Jacob referred had taken place much earlier in Genesis 35:21-22: **"And Israel journeyed, and spread his tent beyond the tower of Edar. And it came to pass, when Israel dwelt in that land, that Reuben went and lay with Bilhah his father's concubine: and Israel heard it..."**

So it is obvious that the area in which Reuben most exhibited his trait of indiscipline is sexual immorality; or more precisely illicit sexual liaisons. Again, does this have anything to do with the country called France today? On the surface, it might not seem so. In fact, many would readily point to a country like the United States as being a hundred times more permissive of sexual immorality than France. However, when you look deeper, you discover something astonishing.

Regardless of the inglorious way in which Hollywood glorifies immorality, the United States still has huge regards for monogamy and near zero-tolerance for adultery, especially among people in public office who are supposed to be role models for the citizens. Sadly, the opposite seems to be the case with France. From the time when the Royalty governed the people, till the present day of republicanism, the issue of adultery is practically an accepted norm, from the leaders to the led. This character flaw seems to be an intrinsically embedded aspect of the national culture of the people, which may not be unconnected to the Reubenic ancestry.

Trace the history of the leaders of France from the beginning to the present day and you will discover that there have always been records of scandals of a sexual nature, whether open or secret. To start with, there was hardly any of the kings of the French nation that was not affected. Even "Louis the Pious" had at least one mistress (Theodelinde of Sens).

In a rather bizarre move, which is unprecedented and which further underscores the point I am trying to establish here, the *Wikipedia* has devoted a special page to list out French royal mistresses, from the time of King Clovis I to Napoleon III. Charlemagne had at least 8 acknowledged mistresses; Henry IV had ten; Louis XIV had at least 19! – which made a writer to note that "Adultery at Versailles seems to have been important politically, and a far more popular sport than horses, tennis, dice or cards."7

Has the story changed in modern times? Not at all. Even the immediate past President of France had his own share – which I need not repeat here without boring the reader with details that are all too familiar. In fact, of Francois Mitterrand, France's longest serving President, it was once reported by *USA Today,* "Throughout his presidency, Mitterrand lived officially with his wife, Danielle, but he spent almost every night with his mistress Anne Pingeot and his daughter, Mazarine, in an apartment across the river from the Élysée Palace."8

This perhaps explains why the French first lady does not have the same official status as her counterpart in the United States. Interestingly, when asked recently if France should formalize the position of the first lady, the former head of France's opposition party, Union for a Popular Movement, Alain Juppe, joked that the country would have to "create a status for the first lady and for the second lady as well."

Let me provide one more example to illustrate my point here. When in 2015, news broke that a certain website in the USA that was dedicated to adulterers was hacked and the details of the members were published online, it became a major story. Many people in the West, who never imagined that such a website could even exist, were scrambling to get a peek into the list to see whether there were familiar names. And the adulterers themselves were so jittery that some began to confess before they were found out.

But what of the French – were they the least bothered about who was there or who wasn't? Hardly. You know why? Here is what a French writer, Anne-Elisabeth Moutet, said on this in July 2015: "We French may have invented the *cinq-à-sept* [French term for a visit to one's mistress], and historically enjoy a particularly relaxed attitude to marital fidelity. In fact conservative estimates suggest that a third of married *citoyens* here have strayed…There are some 300 French-speaking cheating sites…."9

I believe that while the founding fathers of the French nation, as evidence from the country's national symbols has shown, really expected the citizens to constantly wage war against external forces of tyranny, injustice, disunity, mediocrity, and the likes, they might have also unknowingly been echoing another Scriptural message for the French nation if they really hope to take the leading position they were destined to take:

"Dearly beloved, I beseech you as strangers and pilgrims, abstain from fleshly lusts, which war against the soul." (1 Peter 2:11).

France is a nation that is dear to God, and it has in the past waged a number of wars against political oppression and invasion. But how much battle has it fought against moral corruption? Aristotle was right when he said, "I count him braver who overcomes his desires than him who conquers his enemies;

for the hardest victory is over self." So, let me ask again, is the nation of France doing anything to wipe away the stain that set a seal of limitation on Reuben and his descendants or is it instead institutionalizing and justifying it by glorifying fleshly lusts and immoral passions?

To this end, I believe that there is a critical need for the French people to take another serious look at the yearnings and aspirations of their founding fathers as contained in their national symbols and documents. Beyond this, I implore the people to sincerely look inwards with the aim of ascertaining the exact reason that France seems to be lagging behind in all the various areas in which it ought to be taking the lead.

Indeed, there is a need to reflect on why several other nations that came after this blessed country should be excelling far beyond it. And most importantly, there is an overriding need to realize that despite the advances in sciences, civilization and modernization, God remains the brain behind the formation of nations and therefore His principles for sustainable progress and prosperity remain immutable and indispensable.

Finally, I must add that the callings of nations, like the callings of individuals, have certain inviolable conditions attached to them. When such conditions are flagrantly flouted, it becomes practically impossible for the callings to be realized. Moreover, it must be noted that just as callings are different, so are the conditions attached to them. In other words, it is sometimes very risky, if not foolish, to make undue comparisons and conduct one's affairs in line with what appears to be the norm in other places. There are practices that certain individuals or nations engage in that may not have direct consequences on their destinies; whereas, for other individuals and nations, such indulgences only pave way for perpetual limitation and retrogression.

To the French therefore, having clearly established that there is a manifest connection between its historical penchant for immoral passions and its mediocre progress over the years, it is high time to make a collective decision for a total turn-around in national repentance. Let the French nation be aware: there cannot be emancipation from the embargo of limitation while still wallowing in the same mire that brought the limitation in the first place! It is righteousness that exalts a nation; sin is a reproach, not a badge of honor, to any people! (Proverbs 14:34).

CHAPTER SEVEN

GERMANY: THE PACESETTER THROUGH PEACEMAKING

Germany, today, stands tall and strong, not just as a political and economic powerhouse of Europe but also as a "values-lighthouse" for the entire continent and, indeed, the entire world. Although there is a later section of this book that I have exclusively devoted to explaining the necessity of promoting, preserving and propagating national values, the German nation is such that has built a gigantic structure of social, economic, technological and political advancements on the foundations of strong national values and institutions. Consequently, it will be hard, if not entirely impossible, to describe what makes this country exceptional, without delving into the values that are being instilled into and strongly upheld by the citizens.

Let me begin by first pinpointing some of the striking features that qualify Germany to be described as a prosperous nation. As I noted before, Germany's economy is one of the most vibrant in the world. In fact, it is by far the largest and strongest in Europe.

Not only that, the country is also the fourth largest economy in the world and it has continued to grow steadily. In addition, it is ranked 22nd out of 183 countries in the World Bank Group's Ease of Doing Business ranking. In 2014, the country recorded the highest trade surplus in the world worth $285 billion, making it the biggest capital exporter globally. Indeed, Germany is the third largest exporter in the world with 1.13 trillion euros ($1.28 trillion) in goods and services exported in 2014.

Currently, Germany is the driving force of the European Union's economy. Germany's Gross Domestic Product (GDP) is the mightiest in the Eurozone. In addition, German banks act as creditors for many of the banks in other countries, as well as acting as the largest backers, contributing more than a quarter of the funds, for the European Stability Mechanism, the central funding agency that provides loans or credit to European countries in crisis. Recently, when news of crisis in the Eurozone rocked the world, with countries such as Greece, Portugal and Spain running into serious trouble, it was Germany that proved to be the country whose economy could single-handedly stop the Eurozone falling back into recession and the only nation rich enough to save the euro.

What is the secret of Germany's powerhouse status? How could a country that was described as the "sick man" of Europe in the late 1990s and into the early 2000s, suddenly become an economic superstar? Well, to be honest, there was nothing sudden about Germany's rise to prominence. It was an achievement that came as the country committed itself to three key values that distinguish it from many other nations of the world. These values are **diligence, excellence** and **prudence**. Let me explain each of these.

Talking about diligence, I mentioned earlier that Germany is one of the top exporting countries in the world. But one thing is remarkable about this country in this regard – one thing that sets it apart from many other nations and actually enables it to continue to stay strong while several other countries in the Eurozone are begging and crawling their way out of the quagmire of economic recession. This distinguishing quality is that Germany does not meddle so much in simple or basic products that other countries can easily produce; rather, it goes for complex products.

Currently, Germany exports a large portion of the world's most complex products to manufacture; thus making it less open to global competition. It holds a significant advantage over other Eurozone countries that do not specialize in the production of these products, which definitely contributed to its weathering the Eurozone crisis better. According to a 2011 working paper by Jesus Felipe and Utsav Kumar of the Asian Development Bank, 7.93% of Germany's exports are in the hundred most complex products, and only 3.5% of its exports are in the least-complex group of products. On the whole, its top 10 exports include: vehicles, machineries, chemical goods, electronic products, electrical equipment, pharmaceuticals, transport equipment, basic metals, food products, and rubber and plastics.

Why would Germany choose to go the "hard way" in its choice of products to manufacture and export? I tell you the answer. Economic considerations apart, it is a clear reflection of a fundamental part of the national value of the German nation – working diligently to set themselves apart. The attitude of diligence through practical knowledge (not theoretical knowledge as is common in the educational systems of some other nations) is inculcated in German children right from school; so that, as they graduate they are already empowered and equipped to take up daunting production activities.

According to the World Economic Forum's 2012-2013 Global Competitiveness Report, Germany ranks 5th in higher education and training, a factor enabling it to manufacture such complex products; and 3rd in infrastructure, part of what helps Germany move its exports to market so efficiently.

The second thing I mentioned is Germany's commitment to excellence. None can dispute this. Germany is known for its high-quality and long-lasting goods. It is a country that excels in the development of innovative technologies and techniques. "Made in Germany" has been a quality symbol for decades. Consider the German motor industry with its luxury brands such as Mercedes, BMW, Porsche and Audi. The same goes for electronic products and other products from Germany. Their reputation for excellence is unsurpassed! Unsurprisingly, as an analyst has observed, "The country on its own generates 65% of the trade in Europe, which means people want to buy German products in the rest of Europe and all over the world".1

The third secret of Germany is its financial prudence. Put simply, Germans are extremely meticulous about spending, generally, and borrowing, in particular. They love to save, as well as living within their means. Someone once joked that "The German coat of arms features an eagle, but a piggy bank would do just as well..." 2

The BBC, in trying to pinpoint the factors that have strengthened the German economy over years, also reported that "While the rest of Europe gorged on cheap credit throughout the 1990s and 2000s, German companies and individuals refused to spend beyond their means."3 Also, while making a comparison between Germans and Americans, Time magazine reported thus:

"In 2007, the average household in Dallas spent a bit over $54K, including housing, transportation, entertainment, and all-encompassing "shopping." The average German household, by contrast, spent a bit under $34K – a difference of more than $20,000.

Gasoline costs double what it does in the U.S., but on average Germans *spend far less on fuel than Americans ($1,447 annually vs. $2,559 in Dallas), mostly because Germans use public transportation more often. Likewise, there's a gap on household expenditures eating out at restaurants: $1,226 annually in Germany, $$2,662 in Dallas. Overall, while a German household saved 16.7% of disposable income, a Dallas household saved 5.2%..."5*

THE UNDERLYING MESSAGE

As with all the other countries we have considered so far, I have not taken up the trouble of laying bare the distinguishing characteristics of the German nation simply for the sake of eulogizing it. There is an underlying truth that I want to show you. Of all the nations we have so far explored, none appears to be to have had its divine mandate so clearly defined for it as Germany. If the German people are really in doubt of what their calling is, all they need to do is look back at their history to ascertain the points when things have gone so well and the times when there was nothing but catastrophe.

TRACING THE ROOTS OF GERMANY

Let me take you through a few pages of history to make comparisons. For starters, it is important to know that the German nation (which descended from Germania or the Germanic race, as they were called in ancient times) has always proved to be a strong and formidable nation, especially when attacked by external forces. Even before Otto von Bismarck in 1871 united the various tribes and territories that constitute modern day Germany into one nation, the inhabitants had always resisted invasion or subjugation of any kind.

Fair enough, the ancient Germanic people mostly kept to themselves, as their land was divided from the rest of Europe by the Rhine, the Danube and the Elbe rivers. They flourished in their own way, having ingenious understanding of how to exploit and maximize the resources available within their rugged terrain. They were not very keen to allow external influences in their territory; and even though they had only basic tools of warfare, they often succeeded in warding off intruders by employing their most effective war strategy - ambush and guerilla warfare.

Perhaps the most notable demonstration of the Germans' defensive capabilities was at the historic Battle of Teutoburg Forest (c. 9 CE), in which a combined force of Germans, led by Arminius, annihilated an invading Roman army consisting of three powerful legions. The result of that resistance was that the Germanic people remained independent and were never included in the Roman Empire – whereas the surrounding regions, inhabited by the Gauls (encompassing present day France, Luxembourg, Belgium, most of Switzerland, Northern Italy, as well as the parts of the Netherlands) were successfully invaded and Romanized.

That momentous event was indeed a foreshadowing of the strategic role Germany was meant to play in the destiny of Europe, as is being currently witnessed. As Peter S. Wells, author of *The Battle That Stopped Rome* rightly stated, "This was a battle that changed the course of history. It was one of the most devastating defeats ever suffered by the Roman Army, and its consequences were the most far-reaching. The battle led to the creation of a militarized frontier in the middle of Europe that endured for 400 years, and it created a boundary between Germanic and Latin cultures that lasted 2,000 years."6

Corroborating this analysis, historian Herbert W. Benario, emeritus professor of classics at Emory University, said: "Had Rome not been defeated, a very different Europe would have emerged. Almost all of modern Germany as well as much of the present-day Czech Republic would have come under Roman rule. All Europe west of the Elbe might well have remained Roman

Catholic; Germans would be speaking a Romance language…"6

Fast forward to the 20th century, and you would find the same German nation that had seemed invincible, simply by keeping to itself and making the best of its natural resources and abilities – that same German nation had become a warmonger, stirring up needless conflicts and engaging in wanton offensives against other nations. Indeed, Germany was at the heart of the two World Wars that the world has experienced so far. In other words, these wars would not have occurred if the government in Germany on each occasion had not wanted a war.

So, why was Germany so enthusiastic about war? Many reasons have been adduced by historians, but one thing is sure, which I don't think was a mere coincidence: before each of these wars, Germany was at the height of economic and military might. By 1914 for instance, just before the First World War, which ostensibly was triggered in reaction to the assassination of Archduke Franz Ferdinand of Austria-Hungary (an ally of Germany), Germany was one of the countries with the greatest increase in military buildup. That aside, what was known as *Weltpolitik*, or the desire for world power status, was very popular in Germany.

My point is that, while the general impression among historians is that no nation in particular was to blame for the First World War, there was something else underneath. Germany was hungry for power - it has always been - which is what I will be commenting on eventually. Historical researchers have come to the conclusion, after carefully studying the events preceding the War and the way Austria-Hungary was being incited by Germany, that the major cause of the war was Imperial Germany's determination to become a "world power" or superpower by crippling Russia and France.

However, my goal here is not the war in itself but the aftermath. What did Germany gain from the war? Nothing. What did it lose?

A lot! To start with, the country had miscalculated the potential extent of the war. Germany had hoped the war would be a brief and decisive war, like the Franco-Prussian War of 1870-71. Sadly, however, as more and more nations got involved, especially with the German invasion of Belgium in August 1914, it soon became apparent that Germany was not prepared for a war lasting more than a few months. And the loss for the country was catastrophic!

The catastrophe for Germany in that war was all-encompassing. Out of a population of 65 million as at then, Germany suffered 2.1 million military deaths and 430,000 civilian deaths. According to the International Encyclopedia of World War 1, "German losses in World War I were not only a military and demographic phenomenon. To be sure, specific casualties had specific military consequences, and those military consequences had dire political outcomes."

Following the war, Germany was practically stripped of its social, economic and political powers. Before the commencement of the war, Germany had become Europe's most powerful economic and military power, and was second only to the United States in the world. By 1918, however, Germany's economy was in ruins. Germany could not import or export industrial goods and had severely limited trade. Resources and food were diverted to the war. As a result of the war, by 1919, Germany was no longer the second most economically advanced nation in the world.

Moreover, as a consequence of the war, Germany was humiliated, downgraded and exploited in many ways. The climax was the Treaty of Versailles whose 440 Articles demobilized and downsized the military forces of Germany, reduced its lands by 14%, and left 12.5% of the German people living outside German borders. With this treaty, Germany also was stripped of its colonial empire in East Africa. Article 27 stripped Germany of much boundary land, which was distributed to Belgium, Luxemburg,

Switzerland, Austria, Czech-Slovokia, Poland, and, of course, France who claimed coal mines in the Saar Basin as reparation for the mines destroyed in France.

In short, Germany was made to accept full blame for World War I, being required to pay reparations for all the damages done to the allied countries. And that was double tragedy indeed. It was one thing to have been brutally defeated, but it was even worse to be asked to pay reparations to your conquerors. According to Article 231 of the Treaty, Germany had to agree to take full responsibility for the war, which is known as "war guilt cause", and it had to make reparations for the war to the Allied Powers, which amounted to 20 billion German gold marks, worth about $5 billion US dollars in 1920.

Expectedly, the German economy could not take the pressure and it fell apart. In 1921, as Germany could not pay its huge reparations, French and Belgian troops invaded and occupied the Ruhr to take goods and raw materials. This penalty left Germany globally humiliated and bankrupt. So heavy were the war reparations that, by 1932, only about one-eighth had been paid before being suspended by the Lausanne Conference.

Meanwhile, by 1923, as the German economic woes worsened, the country was forced to print more money to pay striking workers. Hyperinflation resulted, wiping out the value of savings. This further wreaked havoc on Germany's social structure and political stability. During that inflation, the value of the nation's currency, the Papiermark, collapsed from 8.9 per US$1 in 1918 to 4.2 trillion per US$1 by November 1923!

Even though the United States eventually came to the rescue when it lent Germany huge sums of money, paving way for the economy to be momentarily rebuilt between 1924 and 1929, the effect of the war lingered, making the Great Depression of 1929 to strike Germany really hard. American loans ceased.

Unemployment soared, especially in larger cities, fueling extremism and violence on the far right and far left, as the center of the political spectrum weakened.

1. The Price of Obstinacy

Now, you would have thought that with all that the German nation suffered during and after the First World War, it would naturally want to steer clear of all forms of conflict. But you would have been wrong! Barely two decades after the war, Germany, again, was at the center of what would turn out to be the most widespread and deadliest war in history, involving more than 30 countries and resulting in more than 50 million military and civilian deaths (with some estimates as high as 85 million).

The German nation, by the mid-1930s, had recovered significantly from the blows of the First World War and made good progress economically and militarily. Headed and instigated by Adolf Hitler, the country began to be puffed up again and pursued aggressive territorial expansion. This began to be demonstrated with gross violations of the Treaty of Versailles.

Hitler's first moves to overturn the Versailles settlement began with the rearmament of Germany, and in 1936 he ordered the remilitarization of the Rhineland. Hitler became bolder as he realized that Britain and France were unwilling and unable to challenge the country's expansionism. Between 1936 and 1939, he provided military aid to Franco's fascist forces in the Spanish Civil War, despite having signed the 'Non-Intervention Agreement'. However despite these highly provocative steps by Germany, including invasion of Austria and Czechoslovakia, other nations that could have haven taken decisive steps to curtail the Germans, did all they could to avoid any confrontation or conflicts, especially through what became known as the policy of appeasement.

As I said before, my focus here is not historical narrative. So,

I'll just sum it up by saying that the Germans, intoxicated by the allure of world dominance and the years they had spent perfecting the use of their new weapons of war - tanks, armored divisions, air power, and above all, the strategy of Blitzkrieg - eventually dragged other nations into warfare. But then, even though it was called world war, it was Germany again that had to bear the brunt of its aftermath.

By the time Germany surrendered to the Allied Forces in May 1945, shortly after the suicide of Adolf Hitler, so much carnage and damage had occurred already and the Germans had to start rebuilding their nation again. That was to be a more daunting task than what happened after the first war. As the Wikipedia reports, "The reconstruction of Germany after World War II was a long process. Germany had suffered heavy losses during the war, both in lives and industrial power. 7.5 million Germans had been killed, roughly 11 percent of the population. The country's cities were severely damaged from heavy bombing in the closing chapters of the War and agricultural production was only 35 percent of what it was before the war."5

Another report had it thus: "The first several years after World War II were years of bitter penury for the Germans. Seven million forced laborers left for their own land, but about 14 million Germans came in from the East, living for years in dismal camps. It took nearly a decade for all the German POWs to return. In the West, farm production fell, food supplies were cut off from eastern Germany (controlled by the Soviets) and food shipments extorted from conquered lands ended. The standard of living fell to levels not seen in a century, and food was always in short supply. High inflation made savings (and debts) lose 99% of their value, while the black market distorted the economy…"6

One thing however is that, as it was after the first war, after Germany seemed to have suffered enough retribution for engaging in another unnecessary war, the country began to rise again economically. With the help of the Marshall Plan (initiated to help rebuild Western European economies after the end of the war), West Germany became an "economic miracle" in the 1950s and 1960s. In fact, after experiencing its *Wirtschaftswunder* or "economic miracle" in 1955, West Germany became the most prosperous economy in Europe. As David R. Henderson, a political analyst and historian, wrote: "After World War II the German economy lay in shambles. The war, along with Hitler's scorched-earth policy, had destroyed 20 percent of all housing. Food production per capita in 1947 was only 51 percent of its level in 1938, and the official food ration set by the occupying powers varied between 1,040 and 1,550 calories per day. Industrial output in 1947 was only one-third its 1938 level. Moreover, a large percentage of Germany's working-age men were dead. At the time, observers thought that West Germany would have to be the biggest client of the U.S. welfare state; yet, twenty years later its economy was envied by most of the world. And less than ten years after the war people already were talking about the German economic miracle."[7]

2. Underlying Message

The truth in all of these events is that therein lies the key message of God to the German people as to the purpose of their calling as a nation. Germany is a nation that is blessed and destined for dominance. All that the people need to stand out is already embedded in their national values. However, this dominance will never be realized through military warfare! Only by seeking and fostering peace will their grandeur continue to shine forth.

Let me emphasize it again. Germany always prospers when it is not fomenting trouble but promoting peace as it is currently doing. I tell you, Germany is currently prospering in all regards as a result of its being part of the Eurozone, which is why it is currently one of the strongest proponents of a united Europe.

So then, we have that glaring evidence again: Germany fares far better promoting peace than participating in wars. Germany's repeated devolution from a great military force to a near annihilated country should consistently serve as a warning. Its current dominant position within the Eurozone has made it clear that, indeed, there can always be a German-controlled Europe, not through traditional warfare and combat but through a rather pacific (howbeit sophisticated) economic means.

REVISITING THE NATIONAL SYMBOLS OF GERMANY

I am not surprised that Germany these days is not so keen about war. It seems to have gradually realized where it's calling, strength and secret of progress lies – fostering and facilitating peace, not spoiling for war.

But then, isn't this the dream the founding fathers of the nation had always nurtured? Was Germany ever meant to be a nation that would be notorious for brazen bloodsheds and mindless holocaust? Let me show you a few messages encoded by the founding fathers in the national symbols of the country.

In the national anthem officially adopted by Germany, here is what you will find:

Unity and Justice and Freedom
For the German Fatherland!
Let us all strive for this purpose
Brotherly with heart and hand!
Unity and Justice and Freedom
Are the Pledge of Happiness;
Bloom in the Glow of Happiness, Bloom, German Fatherland!
Bloom in the Glow of Happiness, Bloom, German Fatherland!

What rallying call is there in this anthem? The call for Germans to seek unity, justice and freedom; to seek the best for their fatherland and to live with a spirit of true brotherliness. That is the only way Germany will ever bloom, grow and prosper.

If you also look at the motto of the German nation, it is the same three words - **"Unity and Justice and Freedom"** – that are repeated. And naturally, "unity" always comes first. It is as if the founding fathers of the nation wanted the citizens to know, from generation to generation, that not only does the progress of the nation depend on the tripod of unity, justice and freedom but that, of these three, unity is number one. Germany must continue to seek and promote peace if it will continue to thrive and excel.

And as I have repeatedly pointed out, the Germans have all it takes within themselves to attain their aspirations to happiness. It is not in aggressively seeking to dominate other nations that Germany will bloom; it is in continuous looking inwards and leveraging the divine blessings of scientific and technological dominance that it already has!

RETURNING TO GOD AND THE SCRIPTURE

Let this message resonate loud and clear. Germany's rise to prominence will always be through ability, not aggression. In particular, the Germans need to take a cue from all that has been discussed in the first part of this book about the place and influence of God in the affairs of nations. God has the power, according to His ultimate program, to raise any nation up to fulfill His purpose. Especially for the German people, the most pertinent scriptural reference that speaks of their situation is found in 1 Peter 5:6:

"Therefore humble yourselves under the mighty hand of God, that He may exalt you in DUE time."

God operates according to His preordained times and seasons.

He has His own calendar or schedule of programs for all nations of the world and it is in the interest of Germany, as it is for other nations, to understand and align with this schedule, so as to be where it is supposed to be at every point in time. As history has continued to show, any attempt to circumvent God's purpose with parochial pursuits will always end in untold devastations.

A PERTINENT OBSERVATION

Now, as Germany continues to enjoy the gains of jettisoning its bellicose past, I am afraid that the German nation is equally losing her moral and spiritual strength. As I travel to Germany and talk to the German people, it is obvious that the Germans of this generation are always afraid of taking a strong position of leadership. The probable reason for this is understandable - two powerful leaders have almost brought the country to her knees.

However, after the Second World War, it is almost as if Germany has been castrated morally and spiritually, especially when it comes to expression of manhood. The only part of Germany that is still functional is the economic aspect of the nation. For me, Germany right now is a pathetic state in leadership and in manhood.

As a matter of fact, it is as if the country has become a totally female-dominated nation. In families, the men seem to have taken a back seat. Same goes for the churches. The fear of giving birth to another Hitler seems to have crippled the leadership potential of the German nation.

I would however like to remind the German nation that apart from powerful and evil men that Germany has produced in the past, it is the same Germany that has given birth to other great men who are great men of God. The Germans who have brought a lot of pain and havoc to the world are normally those in politics, but there have been great men from Germany who have rather contributed positively to our world. Men like Martin Luther, Max Bewer, Reinhard Bonnke, Dietrich Bonhoeffer, Martin Niemöller, Thomas Müntzer, and Andreas Karlstadt. These men were reformers and revolutionaries. They had it in them to conquer and win the world. Generally speaking I think that is the calling of the German nation. The German nation has demonstrated to the world how capable it is to win and capture the world through economics, finances, quality and industry.

I also believe that the reason why Germany has tried to wage world wars is because of the national passion and calling. I believe it is a natural destiny of the German people to conquer the world. However it is not going to be through the weapons of war, but through righteousness and the gospel of the Lord Jesus Christ.

The German nation has proved to the world through their products that they know how to produce what the world needs. The same thing has been proven through the reformation works of Martin Luther and Reinhard Bonnke in Africa. Can you imagine what would happen if the German spirit could be reawakened? The German nation itself is capable of conquering the world for Christ if they are made to believe in themselves and are motivated to launch out with the weapons of the gospel.

However, for this to happen, Germany more than ever before, is in need of a revival. It is my belief that the key to German survival lies in leadership revival. The German nation must be awakened again. The sleeping giant must arise. Another key factor to the German renaissance is the revival and reawakening of men. The men must be empowered again in Germany if the nation is to fulfill her destiny.

Finally, Germany needs a spiritual awakening that will drive out apathy and lethargy that is presently ruling and reigning in the nation. Germans must be made to realize the power of God through the working of the Spirit, instead of only depending on methods and systems. It is my belief that the Lord of creation is waiting for Germany to fulfill her destiny. Just as she led the world in the days of the reformation, the German nation must arise to once again lead the world to gather in the last days' harvest.

CHAPTER EIGHT

UNITED KINGDOM: THE PRESERVER OF ANCIENT VALUES

For four full days in June 2012, fireworks of joy and outbursts of excitement reverberated throughout the United Kingdom (or Britain, as many still prefer to call it) and beyond, in celebration of the 60th anniversary of Queen Elizabeth II's ascension to the throne. In the capital city of London alone, hundreds of thousands of people shrugged off cold and rain, as they flooded into the city to pay tribute to the then 86-year-old monarch. Draped in blue and red colors and waving the Union Jack and placards bearing goodwill messages, the delights of the crowd was unmistakable as they jostled each other to catch the slightest glance of the Queen.

A BBC reporter who covered the event said, "Thousands lined the streets, hung out of windows, climbed lamp-posts to catch a glimpse of their monarch. They stood for hours in a chilly wind wearing daft hats - a metaphor for the attitude of their country. Times are tough, the challenges are great and we respond by cheering an aspect of our culture that, for all its irrationality, is uniquely ours."1

In other countries of the world, millions were glued to their TV screens as they watched the colorful concerts, parades and pageants that characterized the event.

It was the same pomp and global attention that greeted the Queen's 90th birthday (In June 2016), the wedding of Prince Charles (heir to the throne) and Princess Diana (in 1981), the wedding of Prince William (second in line to the throne) and Catherine in 2011, as well as the births of the couples' children.

Regarding the wedding of William and Catherine in particular, it was reported that millions of people in 180 countries watched the event. For most of the spectators and viewers worldwide, it did not matter if they knew the royals personally. They were simply fascinated by the magnetic spectacle of personalities and events connected to the British monarchy. Some were so overwhelmed with emotions that they shed tears of joy.

A MYSTERY WITH A MESSAGE

This extraordinary global appeal of the British monarchy has, over the years, been a curious phenomenon to many observers. After all, many other nations of the world, including Spain, The Netherlands, Saudi Arabia, Belgium, Thailand, Denmark, Norway and Sweden, operate a monarchical system of government; yet none comes close in the level of attention, captivation and prestige that the British monarchy generates. What could be responsible for this?

Some have said that the popularity of the British monarchy outside the United Kingdom is tied to its colonial history; but to what does one attribute the unparalleled devotion of British citizens – including the younger generations and millennials - to anything pertaining to the monarchy? As a matter of fact, a 2012 Ipsos MORI poll found that 79 percent of Britons want to keep the monarchy. Even at the height of the anguish over the tragic death of Princess Diana and the widespread controversy over the perceived role of the monarchy in the saga, a survey still found that about 66 percent of Britons wanted the monarchy sustained.

Similarly, when the first child of Prince William and Catherine was to be born in 2013, numerous well-wishers travelled from all over the UK and beyond to camp outside St Mary's Hospital in west London, where the baby was to be born. They were there for several days before the baby was born. Moreover, shortly after the birth, the UK's *Sunday Telegraph* conducted a survey and found that three quarters of Britons believed that the newborn Prince George would one day accede to the throne to which he is third in line – an indication that they expected the monarchy to continue for a long time.

Even among 18 to 24-year-olds, the age group most likely to hold republican views, the poll showed a solid 69 per cent believed that Prince George would one day become king. Essentially the majority of the country sees no benefit in republicanism, which is the norm in most democratic societies of the world.

The question again is, why does this nation that has witnessed massive changes in all aspects of its national life over the years still cling to this seemingly archaic institution? Why is it that while UK's neighbors such as France were busy carrying out political revolutions that toppled monarchs and demolished monarchies, what Britain was introducing to the world was the industrial revolution instead?

FURTHER ODDITIES

Before demystifying the reason behind the seeming invincibility and increasing popularity of the British monarchy, let me further highlight a few major reasons why the whole phenomenon seems totally unfathomable. First, from a political perspective, the idea of being ruled in a western nation in the 21st century should sound absurd, if not revolting. The trending practice in governance globally is democracy and egalitarianism – to which the monarchy seems antithetical.

Viewed from whatever angle, monarchy is a system which appears at odds with the meritocratic principles of a modern liberal democracy. As Heather Horn, writing for *The Atlantic*, says it, "Nostalgia and the royals' tourist appeal aside, there's something a bit jarring both to logic and to liberal democratic sensibilities about what the queen stands for."2 Someone else asks, "How can a liberal democracy justify power and privilege based on an accident of birth?"1

Second, on the financial side, the British monarchy costs a lot of money to maintain. For starters, the royal family costs the nation a whopping £200 million annually – and that is when there are no special celebrations such as weddings. For instance, just before the coronation of the current Queen in 1952, the UK had been plunged into its fair share of the economic downturn that resulted from the just ended World War II. There was palpable hardship in virtually every community and home in the nation. Yet when it was time for the coronation, there was a general consensus among the citizenry that the glamor and splendor usually associated with the event must never be compromised.

Concerning the event, Mark Easton of the BBC wrote: "Despite post-war austerity, it was decided the event should be a fabulous, flamboyant, extravagant affair with all the pomp and pageantry they could muster. There would be feathers and fur, gold and jewels, anthems and trumpets... Britain - battered, bruised and broke - appeared determined to embrace its monarchy and hang the cost. The paradox is that austerity was positively comfortable with ostentation..."1

Third, on the social side, the monarchy seems averse to the principles of social equity and equal opportunity that most individuals in the global sphere subscribe to. The monarchy apparently embodies and projects a society where some are, by virtue of birth, perceived to be greater and more privileged than others. This, under normal circumstances, is not what most people, even in the UK, would be delighted about. Yet, the British monarchy continues to thrive – and the citizens continue to see it as not just a tolerable but an indispensable social anomaly.

Let me refer again to the coronation of the Queen in 1952 to prove this last point. As a way of ascertaining the true feelings of the populace towards the flamboyant fanfare with which the event was organized, two sociologists, Michael Young and Ed Shils, conducted an extensive survey. In their report which was published shortly after the coronation, they wrote: "The Coronation provided at one time and for practically the entire society such an intensive contact with the sacred that we believe we are justified in interpreting it as we have done in this essay, as a great act of national communion."[1]

It needs to be said though that aside the seeming absurdity of the continuity of the British monarchy, many opponents had actually predicted, over the years, that the monarchy would eventually fall into decline, struggling to remain relevant in the 21st century. Yet, as reports and statistics continue to show, the monarchy has kept on waxing stronger, against all odds. Even those who are opposed to it would tell you that their opposition is just in principle; in practice, it is a different ball game.

So, we return to the burning question: What makes the British monarchy so appealing and indispensable? Why do the people prefer it even when they know that it is outdated, expensive, and dangerous for democracy?

ATTEMPTED EXPLANATIONS

Various attempts have been made to explain why the British monarchy continues to be hugely popular, especially among Britons. Let me list some of the reasons that have been given for the undying power and influence of the British monarchy – then I will show you the real, hidden message in all these.

1. The monarchy serves as a living symbol of Britain's history and heritage.
2. The British love the tradition and spectacle of the royal family, viewing the Queen as a figurehead for the country's values.
3. The monarchy brings in some money, through trade/tourism.
4. While it may seem to offend liberal values like equality of opportunity, it doesn't do any real harm to the nation – so most people don't feel bothered about its perceived excesses.
5. The current Queen, as a person, is a lovable personality, who connects easily with the British people.
6. Uncertainty about what would happen should the monarchy be abolished and the country be left entirely to politicians.
7. The royal family serves as the epitome of Britishness – that is, it embodies the identity of the British nation and has in fact become a global brand for them.
8. Britons are proud of it.
9. The royal family performs ceremonial roles that improve international relations.
10. The British political culture supports it. Political culture is a general attitude, shaped by historical and social experiences, and shared by the majority of the population in a country.
11. The majority of the British people are royalists at heart, not republicans.

12. It serves as an important symbol of the nation, its heritage and its people.
13. Changing the current system of government would be an incredibly complicated process, which would cover almost all British life.
14. It works, and it does so exceptionally – at least, in the UK. Simple as that!

HIDDEN MESSAGE

As I have noted in the previous subheading, the above are just attempted explanations - some of which actually appear plausible. In reality, however, there is something unusual, uncommon and unequalled about the British monarchy and its survival that defies logic; something so grand that makes even its most ardent critics to hesitate in calling for its abolition.

Walter Bagehot in "English Constitution" wrote: "The mystic reverence, the religious allegiance, which are essential to a true monarchy, are imaginative sentiments that no legislature can manufacture in any people."3 Another British writer stated: "In trying to explain the unlikely success of the monarchy, we shouldn't expect the answer to be based on reason. It is not a pocket-book calculation of profit and loss - how much does the Queen cost compared to what she brings in for the tourist trade? The British monarchy is valued because it is the British monarchy. We are an old and complicated society that yields a deference to the theatrical show of society."1

I have read several other comments from Britons from all walks of life and there is a recurrent observation – the reverence and preference accorded the British monarchy defies natural explanations. And this is where the secret lies. There is something about the formation and calling of the British nation that has to do with preservation of ancient values and traditions. Despite being the cradle of the industrial revolution, Britain is a country with a fascinating history and a vibrant heritage. Scattered all over the country are monuments marking its history, from Stonehenge to Buckingham Palace. The country is also home to over 28 cultural and natural UNESCO World Heritage Sites and Heritage Cities including Edinburgh, Bath, Canterbury, Chester and Oxford.

Really, I don't think it is a mere coincidence that contrary to the baby boom in most countries of the world, the fastest growing population in the UK, according to the country's Office for National Statistics, is those between the ages of 85 and above. Nor do I think that it is ordinary that the British monarch sends a personalized card to every Briton who attains a hundred years of age. And most importantly, to return to our main focus of discussion, I do not think that the monarchy in Britain keeps getting stronger and more popular by accident.

And guess what? It is not only the monarchy that is getting better - even the monarch is breaking records! First of all, the current Queen is the longest-reigning monarch in the history of the United Kingdom. Not only that, she continues to achieve feats that none of her predecessors could have dreamt of. For instance, during the ceremonies marking the Diamond Jubilee of 78-year-old Queen Victoria, the only other British monarch to have achieved such feat, she was too frail to make her way down the flight of steps in front of St Paul's Cathedral after the commemoration service. Conversely, however, Queen Elizabeth, despite being 86 years old, gracefully made her way down the same stairs.

Certainly, there must be something about this country that makes it so amenable to the ancient amidst the powerful influence of the wind of modernity blowing within and outside it. The BBC in analyzing this, said: "The British have always chosen the quirks of our history against foreign rationalism. The Romans brought us straight roads and decimalization. As soon as they left, we reverted to impossibly complicated Imperial measures and winding country lanes. The Normans commissioned the Domesday Book to try and impose order on bureaucratic chaos but had to compromise at every turn. That is how we ended up with something called Worcestershire - a place that foreigners find impossible to pronounce, never mind spell."1

The truth I want to show you is that there are certain messages in this eccentric passion for traditionalism that has been innately wired into the British psyche. The enduring influence of the British monarchy, in particular, presents the following strategic messages for the nation of Britain and the world at large:

1. There are national monuments, values, traditions and customs that must never be tampered with, regardless of the pressure of modernization.

There is an unequivocal instruction on this in Proverbs 22:28: **"Do not remove the ancient landmark which your fathers have set."** What this means is that there are some critical aspects of a nation's existence that must remain sacrosanct – because they are meant to perpetually remind the nation of its history and calling. God, who is the grand-architect of nations, takes preservation of national heritages seriously. In Exodus 12, shortly after the Israelites had the first Passover meal, God emphatically told the Israelites: **"And you shall observe this thing as an ordinance for you and your sons forever. It will come to pass when you come to the land which the Lord will give you, just as He promised, that you shall keep this service. And it shall be, when your children say to you, 'What do you mean by this service?' that you shall say, 'It is the Passover sacrifice of the Lord, who passed over the houses of the children of Israel in Egypt when He struck the Egyptians and delivered** our households" (verses 24-27).

Again, in Joshua 4, shortly after the Israelites had crossed over River Jordan, we are told: **"Then Joshua called the twelve men whom he had appointed from the children of Israel, one man from every tribe; and Joshua said to them: "Cross over before the ark of the Lord your God into the midst of the Jordan, and each one of you take up a stone on his shoulder, according to the number of the tribes of the children of Israel, that this may be a sign among you when your children ask in time to come, saying, 'What do these stones mean to you?' Then you shall answer them that the waters of the Jordan were cut off before the ark of the covenant of the Lord; when it crossed over the Jordan, the waters of the Jordan were cut off. And these stones shall be for a memorial to the children of Israel forever"** (verses 4-7).

Let me bring this home. The reason the British monarchy continues to flourish and fascinate, against all odds, is because its survival is crucial to the fulfillment of the calling and destiny of the British nation. Like the Passover feast and the stones in the above Scripture verses, the British monarchy is being upheld by divine hands so that it can continue to stand as a towering fortress amidst the sweeping and scary changes of modernization.

God has so designed the British nation that the monarchy continues to represent the embodiment of its heritage and identity. Daniel Hannan of *The Telegraph* wrote this, soon after Prince George was born: "Ask a friend overseas what he or she associates with Britain and the chances are that the monarchy will come up within seconds. The Crown defines our brand, in the sense that it is thought to say something about the rest of us. Foreign coverage over the past week has been less about the baby than about the way the British are perceived: as traditional, formal, hierarchical, tied to ancient institutions."4

Another person offered this insightful perspective: "Tradition is key to both the Monarchy and the country it is present in. It offers continuity, spectacle and a chance for structured national reflection…Tradition and ceremony are still central to the modern monarchy, with some of Britain's famous patriotic scenes inextricably linked with the royal family. From the most serious, such as the laying of wreaths at the Cenotaph on Remembrance Sunday, to the everyday tradition of Guard Mounting, and from the vibrant military pomp of Trooping the Color to the joyful 'red, white and blue' celebrations of Royal weddings, anniversaries and indeed jubilees, the royal family are very much at the heart of the nation's identity."5

This is basically what every nation on earth needs today – to have their national identity and values so conspicuous in every segment of their national life that they become permanently etched in the consciousness of every citizen (I will be discussing the various strategies for inculcating national values in the citizenry in the concluding part of this book).

What a nation stands for should so reflect in all that pertains to it that no citizen, whether young or old, can avoid being accustomed to it. In this regard, Christopher Hitchens of *The Guardian* (UK) said of the British monarchy: "Nowadays, the royal family is at best something to look at, and at worst something to look away from, or look down upon. It unavoidably remains, however, something to contemplate. The gaze cannot be averted for long. The Windsor clan still compels attention even from the reluctant or the sated. It does so either by pervading the showbiz media, or by occupying the no man's land that separates us from the constitutional future. Whichever direction we may be taking, there is a monarchy-shaped blur that obscures the view. More worrying in a way, there seems to be a fear of what might be revealed if that blur was dispelled."6

However, unfortunately for many nations of the world, this crucial lesson on values which the British monarchy is supposed to convey is seemingly lost on them. For many, especially in Western nations, many of the values upon which the foundations of their nations were laid are being compromised at an alarming rate, in the name of globalization, multiculturalism and political correctness. Ironically, the situation is even more pathetic with the British nation itself. The significance of the monarchy seems to be strictly confined to the throne and all the ceremonies and artifacts attached to it. In other words, aside from the excitement of royal ceremonies and the sense of national pride attached to the monarchy, there is little or nothing of the preservation of national values that the monarchy embodies in the general lifestyle of the majority of the British populace. For some years now, the rates of immoral and criminal behaviors, hooliganism and disrespect for authorities, drunkenness and perversions of all shades in the British society have continued to be a source of concern to many within and outside the country. I will be explaining more about this later on.

2. Nations must seek to establish strong institutions, not strong individuals.

The British monarchy is not just a government or an embodiment of national heritage and identity – it is an INSTITUTION. An institution has been defined as "any public or private structure or mechanism of social order and corporation governing the behavior of a set of individuals within a given human collectivity." Jideofor Adibe, in his paper published in Nigeria's *Daily Trust* of March 7, 2013, wrote: "Institutions are crucial in any system because they help to structure social interaction, allowing for predictability or stable expectations by imposing form and consistency on human activities."

Institutions are said to be identified with a social purpose and permanence, transcending individual human lives and intentions, and with the making and enforcing of rules governing cooperative human behavior. This is why I call the British monarchy an institution. It is an institution that has become solidly consolidated by centuries of experiences and experiments. An institution that has, by its years of stability and endurance, become more tested and trusted than any Prime Minister could ever be.

Writing on the British monarchy as an institution and a trusted upholder of the nation's tradition for centuries, someone said: "Tradition is not just about castles, parades and tourist money. Tradition is an expression of culture, the result of a conversation between governors and the governed that stretches back through time. The solutions that emerge from tradition are very often far better, however superficially strange, than manufactured democracies imposed on societies with no reference to cultural history."[7]

Nations need to spend more time and resources in establishing and strengthening institutions that will help preserve and promote national values and heritage - and where necessary sanctions violators of such values. Let me explain, in detail, why nations need to invest more in institutions than individuals (strong men), using the British monarchy as an example.

- **Strong and independent institutions often outlast strong individuals.** No matter how powerful, effective and resourceful an individual leader may be, their impact is often limited by the duration of their tenure and other related factors. But with institutions, there is assurance of continuity of influence and impact, since they are neither affected by elections nor confined by human frailties. Consider the British society. There had been a number of strong personalities who became Prime Ministers. People like Winston Churchill and Margaret Thatcher readily come to mind in recent times. But where are they now with their reputed fervor and strength of character? Compare them with the Queen who has headed and outlasted 12 governments, both Labor and Conservative, from Churchill to Cameron. That is how institutions work. Strong leaders come and go but strong institutions continue to wax stronger.

By virtue of years of steadiness and experience, institutions offer seasoned solutions to national issues. Having existed for years, institutions have records of facts, statistics and experiences that enable them to be more informed in approaching and tackling societal issues. Beyond that, their knowledge of the workings of government is an invaluable asset to any country. With this, they are able to offer information and suggestions that help governments to make thoughtful decisions. In the case of the UK, even though the Queen has no actual executive power, she retains "the right to be consulted and the right to warn."

- **Strong, independent institutions are more concerned about the broader general interests of the nation and the citizenry.** This sharply contrasts with political leaders who are often beset by partisan politics, parochial interests and the desperation for sustained popularity. The primary concern of institutions is to see that established norms are imbibed, enforced and preserved, regardless of who is involved. They are not fettered by fears of losing re-election or offending certain "godfathers" who may frustrate their plans and activities.

Writing on the British monarchy, in this regard, a contributor on a forum said: "Because the monarchy is not relying on popularity to retain their position, they are in the powerful position of being able to pursue their own agendas without bowing to public pressure. This can be seen rather clearly in the UK, where the Queen and her family control large areas of green land, usually developed as nature reserves or operating farms. Popular vote might want to build on these lands and render them worthless; a politician looking for votes may declare their intention to sell off crown land; but as long as the Queen holds the land, it cannot be built on. Ten or twenty years later, when a surge of environmentalists reach voting age, the land is still there to be enjoyed by all and the politician is likely out of a job."7

- **Strong Institutions are more trustworthy than strong individuals.** Humans are prone to change. Even those with the best of intentions sometimes find themselves in situations where they tend to get either intoxicated with power or distracted and incapacitated by the trappings of office. There have been many cases in history where strong men end up becoming dictators and devourers of national resources. This is why citizens are more inclined to trust an institution that has proved to be consistent and reliable in the pursuit of its mandate for a considerable length of time. Much more than anything else, they know that even when a leader is tempted to stray, institutions exist to remind him of his limits.

Here is how someone describes the regulatory influence of institutions over individual leaders, using UK's example: "Trying to imagine my country without its monarchy, I shiver a little at the thought of politicians being in charge with no-one above them… The monarch's role is to care about her or his subjects from a point of view that most of them don't have, and quietly remind the government (and everyone) that politicians are responsible to a Higher Power, which will stay conveniently in the background as long as they remember the country is not their plaything. To do this while respecting the will of the people as expressed at elections requires, shall we say, an unusual perspective. I never really trust the good intentions of a politician, even one for whom I've voted. But I trust Her Majesty's, so much so that I've never even thought of not trusting her…"7

3. To teach a vital lesson on the uniqueness of national callings.

Here is something that the leadership and citizenry of every nation must be mindful of. As the calling of an individual, together with its peculiarities, is unique to that individual, so it is with the calling of a nation. As with an individual, there are things that work for a certain nation that may not work for another – and this may have a lot to do with the callings of God upon the different nations. To consider the example of the British monarchy, it has withstood the test of time and actually grown better by the day because it is in alignment with the calling of God upon the nation. To put it bluntly, the fact that republicanism works in many other nations doesn't necessarily mean that it will work in the United Kingdom.

In fact, unlike many other nations that have experienced major turbulences in their political history, the British nation with its unique system of government (constitutional monarchy) has enjoyed a long period of resounding peace, stability and progress. And it may interest you to know that the nation had once briefly dabbled into republicanism in the mid-17th century, but the outcome was so disastrous that the monarchy had to be restored.

The bottom-line therefore is that, as the success of the British monarchy, despite pressures and opposition from those clamoring for republicanism, has shown, each nation must know that there are conditions attached to the fulfillment of its calling. Accordingly, in conducting its affairs, emulating other nations and in forming alliances, constant consideration must be given to the primary purpose of its existence.

As I will be showing you later on, deviation from national calling always leads to colossal devastations. With specific reference to the UK's constitutional monarchy, I strongly believe that it should be left the way it is, because there is a powerful purpose for it and there are major messages that it is expected to continuously convey to the British people and to the world at age. As a British writer has reasonably concluded: "Our constitutional monarchy is a result of centuries of tradition – it has taken a thousand political experiments and back and forth between parliament and head of state to arrive at our current system. To throw all that away is to say that our 21st century moral and political sensibilities are so finely calibrated as to trump centuries of cultural evolution. That sounds like the more dangerous course to me."

REVISITING THE NATIONAL SYMBOLS OF THE UNITED KINGDOM

The founding fathers of the British nation and, thankfully, a few other leaders that came after them have ensured that over the centuries, the monarchy and all it represents have been made to become intrinsically woven into almost every aspect of the UK's existence, especially its national symbols. It has been done this way so that dismantling the monarchy will not only be an extremely difficult battle but a very costly gamble.

Take for instance the British national anthem. From the title to the body; from the first line to the last – everything is about the monarchy! Have a look:

1. GOD SAVE THE QUEEN (or the King, depending on the gender of the monarch)

God save our gracious Queen!
Long live our noble Queen!
God save the Queen!
Send her victorious,
Happy and glorious,
Long to reign over us,
God save the Queen.

O Lord our God arise,
Scatter her enemies
And make them fall;
Confound their politics,
Frustrate their knavish tricks,
On Thee our hopes we fix,
God save us all!

Isn't this interesting and instructive? It is all about the monarchy – about preserving ancient traditions and values! Imagine how meaningless and worthless this anthem (which has been sung by generations of Britons for hundreds of years) would be in the absence of a monarch! It would mean that a laborious task of composing and inculcating a new national anthem would begin. But it's not only the anthem that would suffer. What happens to The Royal Mail, the Royal Navy, the Royal Air Force, most of the regiments and corps in the Army, Her Majesty's Revenue and Custom and so on? In fact, someone was so alarmed at the thought that he said, "The expense in new signs and notepaper alone would cripple the government's budget for generations!"

Another message that the founding fathers of Britain seem to be passing on to future generations through the national symbols of the nation is the need to uphold its Christian heritage. The flag of the United Kingdom is particularly revealing in this aspect. It is a merger of the emblems of the three older national flags of the major kingdoms that formed the nation: the red cross of St. George of the Kingdom of **England**; the white saltire of St. Andrew for **Scotland** and the red saltire of St. Patrick to represent Northern **Ireland**. Of course, the emblem of the fourth kingdom in the union, Wales, is not represented in the flag because when the first Union Flag was created in 1606, Wales was already united with England from the 13th century.

Now, don't get confused by grammar. A saltire is simply a cross in a diagonal form. In other words, each of the major kingdoms that formed the United Kingdom had a cross as its symbol. So, in the Union Flag, we have three crosses merged together. Whose crosses? Crosses of Saints George, Andrew and Patrick, who are believed to have been Christian martyrs. And to date, the Union Flag continues to proudly display the crosses. This means that the founding fathers of Britain desired that the nation would perpetually stay true to its Christian heritage.

Why then is Britain no longer proud of its Christian heritage? Why has it become so ashamed to be called a Christian nation and even goes to the point of trying to obliterate Christian principles and practices from its national life? I was deeply saddened the other day when I read an article in one of the British newspapers in which the writer proudly declares, "The country has undergone revolutions, both socially and economically, and the Queen has adapted to the digital age. We are no longer a white, Christian nation…but a multi-cultural nation that inhabits many faiths and cultures."8 This is something to be deeply worried about – which leads us to the next crucial point here. The need to revisit the mind of God for the British nation.

RETURNING TO GOD AND THE SCRIPTURES

Having carefully explored the history and the values of the Great Britain, I want to reiterate that any "progress" that requires dismantling of critical ancient landmarks and demolishing the very foundation on which a nation was founded is a worrisome and destructive one. Particularly for the British nation, the declaration of the Scripture is: **"The hoary head is a crown of glory, if it be found in the way of righteousness"** (Proverbs 16:31). The glory and significance of the monarchy becomes at best superficial and at worst satirical if it has no impact in steering the nation on the path of righteousness and sober reflection.

It is clear, from the history of this great nation, that the Christian faith played a major role in her greatness. A careful study into the Christian history of Britain will show you that monarchy aside, what actually differentiated this country Great from other countries in Europe were the Christian revivals that continuously broke out on the islands.

There is no country in Europe or the world that has experienced the sheer number of revivals, divine visitations and spiritual awakenings that Great Britain has experienced. This began with the heroic activities of Wycliffe and the Lollards who paved the way for Christian reformation in Europe and worldwide. The seed of greatness was planted in Great Britain as a result.

Apart from Wycliffe and his groundbreaking work of spreading the word of God to the British Isles, activities of such men as the Wesleys, Whitefield, John Knox, Tyndale, Fox and others have sown the indelible seed of greatness in the DNA of the British nation.

It is from the British Isles that a lot of revivals were spread to the rest of the world. It is believed that, as at the time when socialist revolution was tearing France apart, it was the revivals taking place in Britain by the reformers that saved Britain from the same bloodshed that had happened in France.

Sadly, since after the Welsh revival, Britain has not witnessed a major national revival. Even though the Jeffery brothers' movement gave birth to the Pentecostal healing revival and the Elim denomination, but that was not enough to shake the whole nation.

It is therefore only reasonable to say that the farther Britain departs from its Christians roots, the more likely its eventual demise. So, just as Britons have excelled in maintaining their conservative nature through their system of monarchy, so also must they be faithful to their Christian heritage.

The calling and purpose of the British nations cannot be denied or erased from history. There used to be a time when people used to say that *"the sun never sets on the British Empire."* Today, however, that saying no longer holds water. I have no doubt in my mind that the departure from God has largely contributed to this. It is a shame to now witness that Great Britain is not even the greatest nation in Europe anymore. It is alarming to see that Great Britain is only number three nation by GDP in the European continent.

On the world stage, one of the former colonies of Britain will soon leave her behind. India is soon to be a bigger economic power than the Great Britain. If care is not taken, by the year 2050, even Nigeria might just as well leave the Great Britain behind in terms of GDP. For Great Britain and her monarch and their greatness not to be reduced to history, I believe they need to return to the place that God has earmarked for them by returning to the preservation of their Christian faith.

I also believe that the paradox of what has happened to England should be a major lesson to all the nations of the world on why no nation should forsake the source of its greatness.

My prayer for the British nation is that Britain will be great again.

PART THREE

ENGRAVING NATIONAL VALUES IN THE CONSCIOUSNESS OF A NATION

CHAPTER NINE

CONNECTION BETWEEN NATIONAL VALUES AND NATIONAL PROGRESS

"Where there is no vision, the people perish…" (Proverbs 29:18, KJV)

So far, we have been able to establish that nations are not formed by accident. There are very cogent reasons for their formations. These reasons are entrenched in the national values that are established by the founding fathers and embodied in the national symbols (the flag, coat of arms, national motto etc.); the national documents (the constitution, declarations etc.) and the national celebrations and commemorations (Independence, Armed Forces Remembrance, Thanksgiving etc.) of every nation.

These values therefore serve as the mission statement of a nation, which the citizens must vigorously and collectively pursue. It is their raison d'etre – reason for existing. It is the bloodstream of a nation. This is why every effort must be made to preserve and engrave these values in the consciousness of the citizens.

Except this is painstakingly done, disaster looms for such a nation.

The central lesson I want to emphasize here is that once a nation loses its values, it is as good as DEAD. It doesn't matter if the nation appears to be existing geographically; it is just a walking corpse. Jesus Christ says, **"You are the salt of the earth; but if the salt loses its flavor, how shall it be seasoned? It is then good for nothing but to be thrown out and trampled underfoot by men"** (Matthew 5:13).

That's exactly the point I am making here. What makes salt unique and useful is its taste, with which it seasons every other thing being cooked. When this taste - this ability to season - is lost, what's left of its purpose? Similarly, when a nation loses its values – the reasons for which it was founded; the features that distinguish it from other nations – of what usefulness is such a nation anymore? On what basis would it even be called a nation, when the essence of its formation is lost?

Again, it doesn't matter if a nation appears to be temporarily prosperous or mega powerful. The fact remains that once its national values are compromised, it is a matter of time – that nation will sooner or later drop dead because it is already being eaten up from within. When the foundation of a building is being eroded, that building may stand for a while but it will eventually collapse.

I will be giving specific examples shortly about some nations. But before then, let me reiterate that national values are to a nation what a mission statement is to a company. A mission statement, according to Glenn Smith, a business expert, is used by business owners "to remind their teams why their company exists because this is what makes the company successful. The mission statement serves as a "North Star" that keeps everyone clear on the direction of the organization."[1]

The moment a company loses focus of its mission statement, it is bound to go downhill. I think this is why most companies have their mission statement glued to a conspicuous location where every member of staff, as well as the owner, can see it often.

This is how it goes for a nation as well. Sadly, I have observed that companies tend to be more concerned about their mission statement than many nations are about their national values. And this is why so many are battling with crippling calamities today. To use the words of Lü Bu-wei, Chinese Prime Minister under Emperor Ying Zheng (in 246 B.C.), "In making judgments, the Early Kings were perfect, because they made moral principles the starting point of all their undertakings and the root of everything that was beneficial. This principle, however, is something that persons of mediocre intellect never grasp. Not grasping it, they lack awareness, and lacking awareness, they pursue profit. But while they pursue profit, it is absolutely impossible for them to be certain of attaining it."

This succinctly sums up the real problems with most nations of the world today. Deviation from the established vision of their founding fathers, to the point that many of the younger generations do not have an idea of the values that set their nation apart!

Before going into details of the importance of engraving national values in the consciousness of citizens, let me quickly cite a few examples to show what happens when erosion of national values is allowed.

DIAGNOSING ROOTS OF NATIONAL DEGRADATION

Throughout the remaining part of our discussion in this book, I will be making specific references to different nations to illustrate and buttress my points. But, understandably, I will be giving particular attention to Nigeria, my native country. The reason, apart from my familiarity with its peculiarities, is because the country is a quintessential national case study in many respects.

NIGERIA

Nigeria is currently going through a plethora of social, economic and political crises that continue to baffle the ordinary observer. But to an enlightened analyst and ardent student of history, there is nothing really surprising about the cataclysmic convulsions presently threatening the stability and survival of the nation.

However, for anyone who is still wondering what the real ailment of Nigeria is – how a country that was so promising at Independence, with many observers predicting great things for the nation due to its abundant natural and human resources; how a country that used to be known as the Giant of Africa, with a booming economy and bubbly populace – suddenly became a beggarly nation, with a battered economy, disruptive polity, dysfunctional institutions, and generally disgruntled populace, I'll give the answer here. Things began to fall apart from the period that the national values that made Nigeria great began to be jettisoned and trampled upon.

What are the national values of Nigeria? I know that many readers would be surprised (as most Nigerians generally) that the country even has national values in the first place. The reason is apparently because these values have been relegated to the background in the national consciousness of the majority of the populace. Truth is, the national values of Nigeria are clearly outlined in Chapter 2 of the constitution of the Federal Republic of Nigeria. In fact, to be precise, that chapter contains the ideals towards which the nation is collectively expected to strive in all ramifications.

Specifically, that chapter of the constitution dwells on fundamental obligations of the government (what the government should take as its central focus); the relationship between the government and the citizens; the political, economic, social, educational, foreign policy objectives and environmental objectives of the nation; interrelationship among the different cultures in the country; obligation of the mass media; ethics of the nation; and duties of the citizens. Beyond that, the chapter lays down the policies which are expected to be pursued in the efforts of the nation to realize the national objectives or ideals.

I will be outlining the specific components of each of the objectives as appropriate; but for now, let me summarize the contents and thrusts of the chapter, using the words of Segun Gbadegesin, as published in the April 29 2016 edition of The Nation:

"Chapter 2 of the 1999 Constitution of the Federal Republic of Nigeria provides a list of our national values, the ideals that we stand for and which government and citizens have a duty to embrace and promote. It reiterates our republicanism, which vests sovereignty in the people with the right to participate in government and the duty to discharge the responsibilities that correlate with that right. We affirm peace, progress, unity and faith as national ideals worth living for and if necessary worth dying for.

We reject corrupt practices and collectively resolve to abolish them from our nation. We pledge to secure maximum welfare, freedom and happiness for every citizen on the basis of social justice. We decide that national wealth will serve the common good and not just a chosen few. We embrace freedom, equality and justice as the foundation of our social order. In other words, no one will be rendered unfree without due process; no one will be treated like a slave or serf; and justice will prevail because these are values that our nation is built upon. They demonstrate our belief in the sanctity and dignity of the human person.

As a mark of our fidelity to these values, we pledge to give every citizen the opportunity to secure adequate means of livelihood under just and humane conditions of work. Our constitution even identifies boldly and unambiguously our national ethic which encompasses all of the above: discipline, integrity, dignity of labor, social justice, religious tolerance and patriotism. From south

*to north, from east to west, and every space in-between, these are the values that
we embrace per the ground norm that binds us as one nation indivisible..."1*

The above are the exact kernels of that chapter of the
constitution. Let me state here that even though I mention the
1999 constitution here, it is simply the amended version of
the constitution that had always been long before then. If you
check the 1979 version for instance, you would find the same
contents mentioned there in the same second chapter. Besides, in
the national anthem, pledge, motto and the coat of arms of the
nation, these same ideals are conveyed. The point I am making is
that there are values that have been clearly defined to be always
upheld and promoted by every citizen of Nigeria – both the young
and the old, the officials and ordinary citizens - in order to make
the nation the pride of the citizens and the envy of other people.

Now, take a look at the Nigerian society today and see if you
will find a single proof that these ideals, especially the ethics
of discipline, integrity, dignity of labor, social justice, religious
tolerance and patriotism, are being upheld and promoted. I tell
you, you will find none! Everywhere you turn, bribery, corruption,
tribalism, nepotism, oppression, brutality, falsehood, dishonesty,
disorderliness, document forgery, age falsification, examination
malpractice, immorality, indecency, religious intolerance, wanton
killings, insurgency and militancy stare you right in the face.

From the citizens, law enforcement agents, institutions, and
the various tiers of government to the socio-cultural groups,
including faith-based organizations, family units and individuals,
the downward slide of the nation's core values is happening at
an alarming rate. As a Nigeria writer once noted, "There was
a time in this country when people of dubious character were
never allowed to associate freely with members of the community.
Parents will not accept money or gifts from their children unless
they are sure of their source of income. Prophets refuse gifts

from people of questionable character…"3 But those days are long gone now. And some keep wondering why national progress and development continue to be a mirage!

In 2001, there seemed to be a temporary awakening that jolted the Nigerian government to the deplorable extent to which the nation had departed from its foundational values. Seeing the abysmal degradation and retrogression that the deviation had inflicted on every segment of the nation, the then President, Olusegun Obasanjo, ordered a special retreat for Ministers and Permanent Secretaries at the National Institute for Policy and Strategic Studies, Kuru, Jos between February 23 and 25. At the end of the retreat, a 12-point declaration was adopted, which has become known as the Kuru Declaration. In essence, the retreat participants declared among other things thus:

1. We subscribe to the New National Ideology, which is, to build a truly great African democratic country, politically united, integrated and stable, economically prosperous, socially organized, with equal opportunity for all, and responsibility from all, to become the catalyst of Black Renaissance, and making adequate all-embracing contributions, sub-regionally, regionally, and globally.

2. We adopt the New Orientation as an agenda for: dealing with immediate and future issues of governance of Nigeria; Removing impediments to efficiency and effective implementation and execution of programs initiated by the Federal Government; and Expeditious actualization of Government objectives and vision of national renewal and re-construction.

3. We rededicate ourselves and those who serve under us to the values of patriotism, honesty, hard work and diligence, merit and excellence, trustworthiness, personal discipline, tolerance and mutual respect, justice and fairness, love,

care and compassion.

4. We pledge to eschew corruption, slothfulness, nepotism, indiscipline, bitterness, prejudice and other manifestoes of ant-social behavior.

5. We shall undertake a critical review of practices and procedures in every Department of Government, so as to rapidly increase their productivity and service delivery to the public;

6. We shall foster a culture of efficiency in the management of funds and other resources; maintaining high standards of resource management; and reducing waste at all times.

7. We shall efficiently supervise all Government Departments and Agencies, ensuring timely returns and reports, and undertaking regular spot-checks;

8. We shall abide by the terms of the Code of Conduct which we all have signed, as expression of our commitment to the crusade against corruption, and working closely with all relevant agencies such as the Independent Corruption Practices and other Related Offences Commission, the Code of Conduct Bureau and the Public Complaints Commission;

9. We undertake to strengthen the partnership in working with the private sector, since this partnership translates to a better appreciation of the wealth-creating capacity of this sector, and the need for Government, through its various ministries and legislative processes, to create an enabling environment for the sector to function efficiently as the major driver of the economy.

10. We shall strive to strengthen and inculcate the culture of working closely and in consultation with the leadership of labor and civil society organizations.

11. We shall mobilize, involve and promote the interest of

all stakeholders, namely, the society in general; since, in the ultimate, all decisions and actions of government are aimed at the promotion of public welfare, there is also the need for a new attitude that has that welfare permanently in focus, as the only goal, and the economic well-being of all citizens, under unfettered freedom, is of cardinal importance; and we shall design strategies and techniques of implementation for the New Orientation so as to ensure that the values being inculcated permeate all levels of management and staff.

The declaration sounded great and promising. But 16 years after, as I have told you already, every resolution seems to have gone down the drain. The values are not taken seriously, simply because they are not considered to be integral to national development. In fact, things have got so bad that people being elected and appointed into public offices are not obligated to be men and women who are adherents and advocates of these values.

How do I know this? Here's a valid proof. Between 2009 and 2016, when ambassadorial and ministerial nominees chosen by the President were screened by the Senate for eligibility, there were occasions when the nominees were asked to recite the national anthem and national pledge. And guess what? Some of them failed this simple test, and woefully so!

Now, that was unthinkable. But, in case you are thinking that such nominees were immediately disqualified as not being worthy leaders, then you're totally wrong! To date, no nominee has ever been disqualified for failing in this regard.

Of course, anyone could be tempted to dismiss this test as not being enough to disqualify a nominee. But let me show you two things that are wrong in this approach by the successive governments. First, in going ahead to confirm the appointments of such nominees, it was being clearly established that knowing the basic national values of the nation is not so important in attaining a prominent position in the country.

In fact, I recall that during the ministerial nominee screening in 2011, a member of the Senate was asked by a reporter whether those who were unable to recite the national anthem would be confirmed as ministers. And the senator replied, "Well, we do not expect that any nominee would not know things like that. This is because we believe that everybody who is a patriot or at least a citizen of Nigeria ought to have those things ingrained inside them. A nominee who is not able to recite simple things like that would not scale the screening process because what it means is that such a nominee is actually not involved in Nigeria. I don't think we would waste time on such a nominee."2

Of course, he spoke the basic truth. But what is the reality? As I said, to date, such nominees continue to get confirmation.

The second and the most disturbing drawback is that it gives the impression to the young viewers watching the televised screening that national symbols, like the national anthem, could be handled with levity. Anyone could have even wondered why, in the first place, the recitation was included as part of the screening process when performance in it would be trivialized at the end of the day. And the nation keeps wondering why its youths are more interested in making money by all means, rather than upholding values of honesty and dignity of labor? Such pretended alarm only wastes time and prolongs problems. The right approach is to admit the root of the problem and tackle it head-on!

USA AND BRITAIN

The United States of America is a country that prides itself on upholding and promoting liberty and human rights. But as I have already shown you, the interpretation of liberty by the founding fathers of the nation has been largely perverted. The liberty that formed the foundation of America was liberty to serve God without restrictions. It was liberty to conduct their lives according to the dictates of the Scripture. Put simply, America was founded on Christian values and principles. Its national symbols and founding documents (The Declaration of Independence; The Paris Peace Treaty of 1783, and the Constitution) clearly attest to this.

The Declaration, in particular, has many references to God throughout the document. The most famous one is that men are endowed by their Creator with certain unalienable Rights. In fact, as I showed you before, the document has this from the very beginning: "We hold these Truths to be self-evident, that all Men are created equal, that they are endowed by their Creator with certain unalienable Rights, that among these are Life, Liberty and the Pursuit of Happiness."

Also, when the Constitution of the country was completed on September 17, 1787, it was signed by the delegates then to be ratified by the states. The delegates signed the Constitution in the "Year of our Lord." This is a direct reference to Christianity. This is found in Article 7 which in part says: "Done in Convention by the Unanimous Consent of the States present the Seventeenth Day of September in the Year of our Lord one thousand seven hundred and Eighty seven and of the Independence of the United States of America..."

And then, when you consider the Paris Peace Treaty, which was the document that formally ended the American Revolution and granted the United States independence from Great Britain, it begins with "In name of the most holy and undivided Trinity." Essentially, therefore, American independence and the founding of the American nation was done in the name of the "Holy and undivided Trinity," which is a concept that is unique to Christianity.

I have gone to such detailed length to show why it is so

incongruous, if not utterly ridiculous, that the American nation in recent times has been trying so hard to disconnect from its Christian roots and values, in the name of modernization, secularization and political correctness. A nation that believed it was founded by the will of God, the Creator, has suddenly begun to elevate Evolution above creationism. A nation that was founded upon the principles of the Holy Bible has suddenly become an endorser and promoter of abortion, homosexuality and transgender rights in the name of liberty.

In fact, things have gotten so bad that Christianity has become an endangered religion and the name of God is fast becoming a forbidden concept in the American society. Prayers to God have been taken out of classrooms since 1962 and Christians are prosecuted for not acknowledging the rights of gays and transgenders. In fact, according to recent statistics, Only 57 per cent of Americans born between 1981 and 1996 identify as Christians; 36 per cent of 'young Millennials' between the ages of 18 and 24 are the so-called 'nones' — they have no religious affiliation at all!

So, how has the American society fared, since it began to deviate from its Christian values? It has been a downward spiral of moral and spiritual disintegration. Let's look at the American society, especially since the landmark U.S. Supreme Court judgment in 1962 that proibited state-mandated prayer in public schools classrooms. According to reliable statistics:

1. For 15 years before 1963, pregnancies in girls ages 15 through 19 years had been no more than 15 per thousand. After 1963, pregnancies increased 187% in the next 15 years.

2. For younger girls, ages 10 to 14 years, pregnancies since 1963 are up 553%.

3. Before 1963 sexually transmitted diseases among students

were 400 per 100,000. Since 1963, they were up 226% in the next 12 years.

4. Before 1963 divorce rates had been declining for 15 years. After 1963 divorces increased 300% each year for the next 15 years.
5. Since 1963 unmarried people living together is up 353%
6. Since 1963 single parent families are up 140%.
7. Since 1963 single parent families with children are up 160%.

Whether this alarming statistics is actually related to the ban on prayer in classrooms is not my focus here. My ultimate concern is to show the disturbing moral free-fall and general discontent that continue to be a prominent feature of the American society since it began to contest its Christian roots. Check out rates of suicides, for instance, and you will be astonished. As a matter of fact, the CDC's National Centre for Health Statistics recently reported that suicide rates in the country are the highest they have been in three decades, increasing 24 percent between 1999 and 2014.

But perhaps the most glaring consequence of America's deviation is the unending spate of gun violence and mass-shooting that occurs almost daily. In 2015 alone, there were 64 school shootings, according to a dedicated campaign group set up in the wake of the Sandy Hook elementary school massacre in Connecticut in 2012. That same year, some 13,286 people were killed by firearms, while about 26,819 people were injured.

Observing the seemingly hopeless trend of gun deaths in America, even the immediate past president, Barrack Obama, was brought to tears On January 6, 2016, while talking about the mass shooting at Sandy Hook elementary school, which claimed the lives of 20 children and six adult staff members. His tears were not just in empathy with the family of the victims but also a demonstration of his helplessness at the situation. He had done everything possible to ensure that gun control laws were put in place, but gun lobbyists always seemed to prevail upon the Congressmen, a sign that the center can no longer hold.

Indeed, America is increasingly becoming a restless, insecure and paranoid society, being eaten up from within and threatened from without. And this makes me ask again, would the situation had become this bad if the citizens had not deviated from the vision of their founding fathers?

This same trend of deviation from its founding values and principles - together with the inevitable consequences - is evident in the British nation. The same British nation that produced countless revivalists and missionaries that took the Gospel to different nations of the earth, has, in the name of encouraging a multicultural society, destroyed most of its Christian and cultural roots. Alarms are being raised at the speedy rate at which Christianity is dying out of Britain – to the point that some analysts have predicted that, by 2067, Christianity would have become extinct in Britain!

Here is a recent report from a British newspaper, The Spectator: *"It's often said that Britain's church congregations are shrinking, but that doesn't come close to expressing the scale of the disaster now facing Christianity in this country. Every ten years the census spells out the situation in detail: between 2001 and 2011 the number of Christians born in Britain fell by 5.3 million — about 10,000 a week. If that rate of decline continues, the mission of St Augustine to the English, together with that of the Irish saints to the Scots, will come to an end in 2067. That is the year in which the Christians who have inherited the faith of their British ancestors will become statistically invisible. Parish churches everywhere will have been adapted for secular use, demolished or abandoned."*3

WHY NATIONAL VALUES MUST BE PRESERVED AND PROMOTED

As I have variously illustrated above, the first reason national values must be engraved in the consciousness of citizens is that, except this is done, a country loses its identity and begins to die gradually from within. It equally becomes exposed to cultural invasion and systematic extermination of its founding values. There is a lot of this going on in Nigeria currently. But for now, let me focus on some Western countries as my case study.

I think the main problem with most countries founded on Christian principles, especially in Europe, is that they are far too LIBERAL and too FICKLE. Multitudes of people from diverse cultures and with different religions troop into these countries every year. Sadly, nothing much is done to ensure that these immigrants conform to the traditional values and ideals of their host nations. Even something as simple as learning the language of the host nation is not encouraged. In fact, in some worst cases, these people are allowed to take a portion of the country to themselves and are allowed to form their communities and freely practice their native traditions, some of which may run contrary to the ideals of the host nation (forced marriages and female genital mutilation are good examples). What you get in the end is a cacophony of values, leading ultimately to chaos and conflicts.

Britain is a clear example of this. There are communities of people from different cultures of the world, who are not ready to integrate into the British society. In fact, there are certain places you go in Britain and you would think you were in another continent entirely. And yet the British society allows these people to enjoy all kinds of privileges and benefits just like any other British citizen. What has this led to? The destruction of the traditional values of the British society, as these foreigners continue to multiply and demand for more rights and privileges (it's in the nature of humans to do this!).

Not only that, as more foreign nationals hear or observe that it is possible to enjoy maximum benefits in a host nation like Britain, while still holding on to your beliefs and practices, they are further encouraged to do all they can to rush into such a country. What caused the migrant crisis in Calais, which saw would-be immigrants employing all sorts of means to force their way into Britain? Why are multitudes of African immigrants risking their lives across the ocean to get to Europe in overcrowded boats? Why are migrants from war-torn Islamic countries such as Syria and Afghanistan not going to other Islamic countries but prefer European countries, despite knowing that there are cultural differences?

Yes, I know it's because they want a better life; but it's not just that – it's also because they know that they can have this better life, almost at no cost. They can retain their traditional values and beliefs, which may be opposed to those of the host nation, while still enjoying the benefits that the nation has to offer – thereby enjoying the best of both worlds!

The recent incursion and onslaught of different terrorist groups has further exposed the foolishness of multiculturalism and compromise of national values in Western nations. When people are left to hold whatever beliefs they want, without the government making conscious efforts to ensure that these beliefs align with the collective ideals of the nation, it becomes easy for such people to constitute themselves to enemies within; or in the worst scenario they simply collude with external enemies to wreak havoc on their supposedly adopted nation.

The birth of homegrown terrorist groups and the rate at which supposed citizens of certain Western nations are trooping out to join deadly terror groups, such as ISIS, has further validated this truth. And it doesn't stop at that. As the true citizens of these countries equally observe that "outsiders" are allowed to invade their countries and trample on their customs and traditions, they are sometimes forced to resort to aggressive agitations and violence, as a way of expressing their displeasure. This is the current situation in Europe, as confirmed by the Foreign Affairs magazine of March/April 2015:

"Thirty years ago, many Europeans saw multiculturalism—the embrace of an inclusive, diverse society—as an answer to Europe's social problems. Today, a growing number consider it to be a cause of them. That perception has led some mainstream politicians, including British Prime Minister David Cameron and German Chancellor Angela Merkel, to publicly denounce multiculturalism and speak out against its dangers. It has fueled the success of far-right parties and populist politicians across Europe, from the Party for Freedom in the Netherlands to the National Front in France. And in the most extreme cases, it has inspired obscene acts of violence, such as Anders Behring Breivik's homicidal rampage on the Norwegian island of Utoya in July 2011. How did this transformation come about? According to multiculturalism's critics, Europe has allowed excessive immigration without demanding enough integration—a mismatch that has eroded social coesion, undermined national identities, and degraded public trust..."4

In realization of the dangers of multiculturalism (which many would consider belated), some European leaders have begun to take frantic measures to see how to undo some of the damage that has been done to their national values and identities. Shortly before his recent resignation as Prime Minister of Britain – which incidentally was caused by the majority of British citizens expressing displeasure at the fact that being in the Eurozone was eroding their national identity – David Cameron admitted in regret: "We have lacked the confidence to enforce our values ... No more turning a blind eye on the basis of cultural sensitivities."5

He didn't stop at that. He actually went ahead, in early 2016, to unveil a set of policies that seek to convince immigrants to assimilate into British values, or at least integrate culturally. One of these was a 20-million-pound initiative to teach an estimated 230,000 Muslim women living in Britain who speak little or no English to master the language.

Following the same pattern, in Germany, Labor Minister, Andrea Nahles, wrote her own column in the *Frankfurter Allgemeine Zeitung* that refugees who refuse to integrate or learn German faced having benefits cut. "Whoever comes here to seek refuge and begin a new life must adhere to our rules and values...We will cut the benefits of those who send the signal that they do not want to integrate. From my point of view, that should also be connected to participation in language courses and, in addition, adhering to the basic rules of our coexistence."[6]

Perhaps the most vocal expression of the present disillusionment of most European leaders and citizens is the one that was conveyed in an interview granted by former French President, Nicolas Sarkozy, a "repentant" multiculturalist. He said it emphatically, "If you want to become French, you speak French, you live like the French. We will no longer settle for integration that does not work, we will require assimilation... Once you become French, your ancestors are the Gauls. 'I love France, I learned the history of France, I see myself as French'," is what you must say."[7]

The second and more important reason that national values must be engraved in the consciousness of the citizens of a nation is that the greatness of a nation is hinged on its continued commitment to its foundational values. Where national values are compromised or neglected, national development becomes an uphill task and the nation becomes infamous for corruption, perversion and retrogression.

Isn't this the real reason a country like Nigeria remains prominent on the list of countries with poor living standards, life expectancy, infant and maternal mortality, as well as other indices of national progress? Isn't this why the massive national allocations and international aids poured into the country every year achieve little or no result at the end of the day? Isn't this why it appears nothing is working at all in the nation?

It is true that the present government of Nigeria is making some efforts to bring noticeable transformations in all segments of the Nigerian society but without crucial and consistent emphasis on the national values that should govern the thinking, actions and aspirations of every citizen of the nation, nothing much would be achieved.

The message here is that the issue of ethics and core values must be taken very seriously by any nation that is really desirous of greatness and invincibility. It is the foundation and fortification of any society. It gives character and direction for its peoples. Commitment to national values will help bring about the much needed national development where saboteurs do not exist. This is one reason I have been advocating for national reorientation, particularly on national values, in countries like Nigeria.

Some people may not know it, but Nigeria had not always been the way it is now. There was a time when Nigeria was the envy of many other nations. There was a time when Nigerians were not scrambling to get out of the country to become second class citizens of other nations. There was a time when citizens of other nations, particularly African nations, were trooping into Nigeria, which to them was a safe and comfortable haven. Many people do not know the origin of the "Ghana-Must-Go" bags that are so popular in Nigeria now. They may not know that the influx of Ghanaians got so much at a time that there were protests that they needed to return to their homeland. The question is, why did the Ghanaians come rushing into Nigeria in such a large number in the first place?

Many people may not know that there was a time when the naira, which has become so terribly inferior to the dollar, was at a time much higher in value than the pounds sterling, not to mention the dollar. And I'm sure that not many would know that there was a time in Nigeria that, without oil money (which sadly has become the dominant factor in the direction of the Nigerian economy), certain segments of Nigeria enjoyed free education, free health services, rapid infrastructural developments and remarkable technological advancements.

But then, where is the country today? What happened to the popular Groundnut Pyramid in the north? What happened to the cocoa plantations in the west? What happened to the oil palm and rubber plantations in the east and west? How much is the country generating from these today? Virtually nothing – because these erstwhile features of the national life of the people, which were driven by commitment to the values of hard work, dignity of labor, self-sacrifice, discipline and so forth have been corroded and replaced with materialistic propensities, fuelled by the "get-rich-quick" syndrome that permeates every segment of the present generation of Nigerians.

As Segun Gbadegesin, whom I quoted previously, has noted: "In the colonial era and in the post-colonial and pre-military era, there were veritable institutions that took on the responsibility of inculcating national values with dedication and commitment. Discipline was enforced in schools and religious institutions. This translated into a productive workforce and a patriotic citizenry. We remember the teachers that made us who we are and the pastors and imams that lived penurious lives but delivered the words of truth without fear or favor. They are hardly here anymore."[1]

My point is that a government may invest so much and work

so hard towards national advancement, but if the catalyst of national orientation is left out, the change may be a mirage. Indeed the orientation and change must start with the self. Nigerians must be encouraged to reinvent their collective sense of values, attitude, and social order. Let me repeat it - no matter the amount of reforms undertaken by the Nigerian government, the nation will never be great until value reorientation is vigorously pursued. The Nigerian value system as it stands today is in shambles and there can be no meaningful progress until this is visited.

Imagine what would have happened if the great declarations made at Kuru were followed to the letter. Imagine what Nigeria would have become today. Let's be realistic. There is no need to re-invent the wheel to make Nigeria great again. Money was spent and brilliant recommendations for restoration of Nigeria through attitudinal change were put into the Kuru document. Unfortunately, poor commitment to policies, which is the greatest limitation of all Nigeria's grand policies, struck and the country remains stuck.

Nigeria needs to take the issue of promotion of core values and ethical ways of doing the right thing most seriously and push the acceptance of same with similar seriousness that economic and public sector reforms enjoy. Nigerians must learn to value hard work, integrity, honesty, and accountability over financial gains. The social sins that Moandas Karamach and Gandhi made popular must be eradicated in the Nigerian society. These sins - which are: Wealth without Work, Pleasure without Conscience, Science without Humanity, Knowledge without Character, Politics without Principle, Commerce without Morality, Worship without Sacrifice - are problems that Nigeria must deal with.

Any attempt at restoring the fallen Nehemiah walls of Nigeria must accommodate value reorientation; otherwise today's predicament will not only remain but continue to fester. Studies have revealed that when national life is taken over by social sins, the citizens will inevitably pursue wealth without work, knowledge without character, pleasure without conscience, commerce without morality, worship without sacrifice, science without humanity and politics without principles.

However, with re-orientation on national value system, there will be respect for human life and corporate values. The youth will imbibe the culture of loyalty, honesty, integrity, patriotism, hard work and productivity, wealth creation, employment generation, entrepreneurship, intangible wealth and competition.

Beyond the youth however, the generality of Nigerians will learn to value hard work, integrity, honesty, and accountability over financial gains. They will learn to believe in themselves positively and see the country as their collective asset and commonwealth to keep in trust for generations. In addition, Nigerians will begin to appreciate and support made-in-Nigeria products and brands. Naturally, economic growth and attraction of foreign investors will follow because national security will be assured. Unemployment figures will drop drastically and opportunities will abound for self-employment, creativity and so on.

Let me add however that any efforts made towards teaching or re-orientating Nigerian citizens on national values must strictly consider the following, among other crucial issues:

- An overview of Nigeria's value system.
- The roles/effects of the social media, educational institutions, public and private organizations towards re-inculcating values.
- Methodology to reach every Nigerian to understand and radically change the culture, values and belief system.
- Redefinition of what it means to be a Nigerian.
- Impact of Nigeria's current situation on the Nigerian's psyche and the economy.

- A roadmap to ensure that every Nigerian accepts and imbibe this critical reawakening on national values.

In the succeeding chapters, I will be looking in-depth into the ways by which the educational system, the media, religious organizations and civil societies can specifically help in preserving and promoting national values among the citizenry. I am particularly delighted that the present government of President Muhammadu Buhari has begun taking commendable steps in this direction of reorientation on national values with the recent launch of the "Change Begins With Me" campaign on September 8, 2016.

According to the government, the campaign is aimed at establishing the values of accountability, integrity and positive change in the attitude of Nigerians. Speaking on the launch, Nigeria's Minister of Information, Alhaji Lai Moammed, said, "We believe that what is wrong with Nigeria is not limited to the elite, the political class and the civil service; if we want that change, therefore, it must address all the issues and target every strata of the society."8

Lending his voice in explaining the essence of the campaign, the Director General of the National Orientation Agency, Mr Garba Abari, said in an interview, "The Fight against corruption must not begin with the government; people must be in the vanguard of fighting corruption. Our schools, roads, hospitals should have been better than what they are now, but corruption has stalled their development. What would you say about a woman who uses chemical to forcefully ripen banana and sell it to the public? What about a woman who would use a padded `mudu' to sell rice? A petrol attendant who would claim not to have change so that the buyer would leave the change - all these are corruption…We, the citizens, must take a second hard look at what we did wrong that we will not do tomorrow. The change must start with the people in the little things they do in their families, place of work and responsibilities." 9

As I said before, this is a step in the right direction, and it provides a positive roadmap for national development and national integration, provided there is sufficient enforcement and adherence to the tenets. Already, discerning Nigerians are beginning to throw their weight behind the campaign, knowing the ripple benefits it will bring to the nation, if imbibed. The Nigerians in the Diaspora Monitoring Group (NDMG), for example, stated that the campaign offers the last hope of restoring respectability to Nigeria and Nigerians abroad. According to them, "Any Nigerian who has travelled outside the shores of the country would attest to the stereotyped perception of Nigeria that is largely negative because of the ills committed by a few. A widespread adoption of the 'Change Begins With Me' campaign would bring about more individuals changing their ways at personal level, which would then multiply to present a positive image of the country."10

THE GERMAN EXAMPLE

Just before I move on to the next chapter, let me briefly take you away from Nigeria to see a good example of how inculcation of national values in citizens can contribute significantly to national greatness.

Recall that I mentioned earlier, while dwelling on the calling of Germany as a nation, that Germany is currently an economic superpower in Europe. It may interest you to know that one of the key secrets of Germany is its addiction to saving and aversion to borrowing. Germans are naturally thrifty – and this is deeply entrenched in their national life and consciously inculcated in their citizens. This naturally makes Germans discipline themselves to live within their means.

The interesting thing is that Germany's extreme aversion to debt is even rooted in the German language itself. According to

Prof. Marcel Fratzscher, head of Germany's leading Economic Research Institute, "The German word for debt - 'schuld' - is the same as the German word for 'guilt'. To get into debt you have done something bad and that describes the German people's attitude quite well."11

Unlike what happens in many other nations that are given to materialism and consumerism, Germans don't feel the need to be ostentatious because there is no pressure on anyone to show off. They prefer to save for the rainy day – and this attitude flows from the leadership to the citizenry. In 2015, the BBC went to the streets of Berlin to find out the attitude of Germans to money. Here is an extract from their findings:

"On the streets of Berlin young Germans told us what they would do if they won a million euros. A new car, a holiday, a new outfit? "I would save it for when I need it," came a typical reply."11

Are you still wondering why such a country can easily survive economic meltdowns that are crippling nations around them? Are you still wondering why a materialistic nation, like Nigeria, with all its resources, is still far behind a country like this? National values can never be separated from national greatness!

CHAPTER TEN

NATIONAL VALUES AND THE EDUCATIONAL SYSTEM

O ne of the most effective ways to instill national values in the consciousness of a nation is to target its younger generations through the educational system. Children all over the world spend a greater deal of their time in school settings. Besides, people generally spend a lengthy part of their early life (sometimes up to 16 years!) getting formal education in a structured setting. Imagine what these many years of focused, consistent and practical teaching could do to the mentality and psyche of the average citizen of a nation!

Some years back, a psychologist, Stanton Samenow, and a psychiatrist, Samuel Yochelson, sharing the conventional wisdom that crime is caused by environment, set out to prove their point. They began a 17-year study involving thousands of hours of clinical testing of 250 inmates in the District of Columbia, United States. To their astonishment, they discovered that the cause of crime cannot be traced to environment, poverty, or oppression. Instead, crime is the result of individuals making, as they put it, wrong moral choices. In their 1977 work, *The Criminal Personality*, they concluded that the answer to crime is a "conversion of the wrong-doer to a more responsible lifestyle."[1]

Also, in 1987, Harvard professors, James Q. Wilson and Richard J. Herrnstein, came to a similar conclusion in their book, "Crime and Human Nature." They determined that the cause of crime is a lack of proper moral training among young people during the morally formative years, particularly ages one to six. This is why the school environment, which allows for unrestricted monitoring, mentoring, audio-visual teaching/learning aids, amplified by peer group influence and good discipline, provides a most conducive atmosphere for instilling the foundational values and ethics of a nation.

Whatever the mind absorbs at this early stage of life invariably becomes a part of it almost all through life. If citizens can become very familiar with what is expected of them as crucial members of the society at this stage, many of the deviations and delinquencies that we observe in many societies today would be drastically minimized because it is these same youngsters that eventually grow up to hold key positions of leadership in all segments of the society. I believe this was why Albert Einstein, the renowned scientist, once declared, "One should guard against preaching to young people success in the customary form as the main aim in life. The most important motive for work in school and in life is pleasure in work, pleasure in its result and the knowledge of the value of the result to the community."

TRANSFORMATIVE EDUCATION

The educational system of a nation at all levels must be tailored towards total, transformative education. Transformative education is one that goes beyond just the **head** (cognitive and intellectual mastery) but affects the **hands** (skills acquisition and entrepreneurial orientation) and the **heart** (good character formation). It is this kind of holistic education that prepares and positions young people to become not just successful but responsible members of the society who conscientiously uphold and promote national values and ethics wherever they find themselves.

Wangaard D. et al (2014) describe transformative education as one that "is focused on the broader goal of promoting positive youth development with an ethical lens. It is the deliberate use of all dimensions of school life to have students and adults able to ethically analyze and evaluate academic material and life and choose to demonstrate pro-social character. This comprehensive approach utilizes every aspect of schooling — the content of the curriculum, the process of instruction and professional development to support it, the quality of all relationships, the handling of discipline, the conduct of co-curricular activities, the outreach to parents and community and the ethos/climate of the total school environment — which seeks to foster good character in all school members."2

I am glad that governments all over the world are beginning to wake up to the power that the educational system has on instilling values. For instance, Australia's Adelaide Declaration on education, says: "Australia's future depends upon each citizen having the necessary knowledge, understanding, skills and values for a productive and rewarding life in an educated, just and open society. High quality schooling is central to achieving this vision. … Schooling provides a foundation for young Australians' intellectual, physical, social, moral, spiritual and aesthetic development".3

Having understood the directions and metamorphosis of educational objectives in the 21st century, it is important to highlight the specific ways in which education can be used as a tool for instilling national values and ethics in the citizenry, right from school age.

THE APPROACH

In instilling values into citizens through the education system, it is essential to consider the contents of the curriculum and the focus of extra-curricular activities in schools. With regards to the curriculum, one indispensable strategy of making national values an integral part of the thinking and behavior of the citizens is making History a compulsory subject in schools. And by schools, I mean right from elementary school, using methods and techniques that are appropriate to the pupils' understanding.

Why do I think History is so important in schools? History as a subject serves as a bridge between the past and the present. It connects citizens to the passions and sentiments of their forefathers. History lets citizens know the reasons why they are the way they are. It links the burden of the past to the concerns of today. No wonder people say any nation that doesn't know her history doesn't have a future.

Moreover, History gives a sense of national identity by providing citizens with a context from which to understand themselves and others. It helps them understand change and societal development by providing information on the emergence of national institutions, problems, and values. Beyond that, it improves citizens' decision-making and judgment by showing them models of good and responsible citizenship. It reveals the great men and women of old who successfully worked through moral dilemmas, as well as ordinary people who provide lessons in courage, diligence, or even constructive protest. History equally teaches students how to learn from the mistakes of others.

The sobering truth about history generally is that there is never total silence about it – if the right source does not tell it, the wrong source will. What I mean by this is that if the government of a nation does not consciously include History as a subject to be compulsorily learnt by students, these inquisitive and impressionable minds will learn the history of their nation or ancestors anyway, especially from movies and other sources.

Unfortunately, what most of these external sources portray are either distorted or commercialized versions of history. Movie makers in particular are primarily businessmen and their number one consideration in deciding which story to dramatize or the angle from which it should be dramatized is PROFITABILITY. And so, it will be a great disservice to assume that since many movies are available on history, it may not be necessary to make it History a must in schools.

Fortunately many countries of the world have made History an integral part of the school curriculum. Sadly, however, some countries like Nigeria seem to be alarmingly ignorant of the importance of History in schools. The case of Nigeria is particularly worrisome. Over the years, History as a subject has been seen as inferior to many other subjects and actually dispensable. Currently, it is one of the subjects with the least attention in Nigerian schools and consequently most students don't consider it necessary.

As Professor Alice Jekayinfa, President of the History of Education Society of Nigeria, has noted, "History as a discipline has been relegated in Nigeria whereas the discipline is the bedrock of any nation."4 The most disturbing aspect is that, currently, following a recent restructuring of the Nigerian school curriculum, History, as a subject, has been practically removed.

Let me categorically declare that this systematic extermination of History in the Nigerian school curriculum is a FUNDAMENTAL FLAW in the Nigerian educational system. Having previously highlighted the importance of national values to the identity, stability, prosperity and continuity of a nation, I'm not sure that there is need for me to explain the point I have just made that relegating History in Nigerian schools is a recipe for national disaster.

Is it any surprise that many young Nigerians have no knowledge of the values and ethics of the nation, much less abide by them? Is it any surprise that they do not know significant national days, monuments, symbols and their significance? Is it any surprise that the national anthem and national pledge are sung either half-heartedly or as a form of entertainment? And worst of all, is it any wonder that patriotism, tolerance and a sense of pride in national identity are lacking?

The mistake currently being made by policy-makers in the Nigerian educational system is to think that History can be replaced by subjects such as Social Studies, Civic Education and Government. Unfortunately, these subjects, unlike History, are mainly concerned with present and static realities. They have nothing to do with the progressive evolution of a nation or the major events and symbolisms that have come to define the people and their values.

Cheeringly, some prominent individuals and groups in Nigeria have begun clamoring for the restoration and elevation of History in the Nigerian school curriculum. Just recently, national leader of the All Progressives Congress party, Asiwaju Ahmed Bola Tinubu, during a public review of the book, *Muhammadu Buhari: The Challenges of Leadership in Nigeria*, on October 3rd 2016, briefly made a strong case for the return of History as a subject in the Nigerian school curriculum, saying any nation which forgets its past has lost a beacon to guide its actions. In his words: "If countries, including United States of America, teach their students about their history, why not Nigeria, with its rich history and tradition? History helps a people to connect with the past and learn from past pitfalls."5

SIGNIFICANCE OF ROLE MODELING AND ROLE PLAY

Now, having mentioned the importance of revisiting school curriculums, with particular emphasis on giving maximum attention to History as a subject, I must state it clearly that the focus of teaching this subject must go beyond theory. The reason many students have issues with History as a subject is because of excessive emphasis on the academic approach – presenting it as a mere academic subject that must be studied and passed in examinations.

As a scholar has observed, "Students' knowledge of history has suffered because of untrained teachers, reduced course requirements, and textbook treatments that are bland and voiceless and directed more toward trivial coverage of details than to the fullness needed to bring vitality and credibility to events of the past."6

The point is that efforts must be made to make History topics practical, lively and impactful. To achieve this, two things are essential: Role modeling and role playing. By role modeling, I mean that students must see that the lessons, precepts, principles and values that they are being taught are being upheld and followed by older persons around them. Youngsters learn faster by examples than by mere teaching. And so, as they observe the seriousness with which school staff, parents, national and community leaders take issues regarding national values and symbols, they will understand their significance better.

Let me quote Gbadegesin again, "If we are to inculcate national values, there must be instructors and role models for that purpose. But genuine instructors are lacking not because there are no expert teachers of values, but because, there is more to instruction and role modeling than rote teaching and learning. A role model sets a pattern of behavior that is emulated by the followers."

Role-playing, on the other hand, has to do with real time dramatization of some of the historical events that are peculiar to a nation. Students can be placed in groups and made to enact the roles played by the key historical figures of a nation. This will make the events more real to the pupils, as well as encouraging them to study more about the events and imbibing the qualities of the heroes represented.

According to Dr Joe Merton of the Department of History, University of Nottingham, roleplay activities help in deepening student learning and breeding historical understanding and empathy. In his words: "They make the past immediately accessible to students – a felt experience or reality, because they themselves are participating in it via the roleplay – and stimulate student enthusiasm and motivation for the topic under discussion. They capture the sheer complexity and difficulty of history, and the complex, often morally challenging questions it poses for us. They aid students' academic progress and understanding by stimulating deeper learning of the historical topics under discussion…And they develop students' empathy with historical actors, events and experiences, and therefore the past more broadly, furthering historical understanding – which is surely what studying History should be all about."7

It is my belief that if the underscored approaches and strategies are adopted and implemented with all seriousness, the truism of that verse of Scripture in Proverbs 22:6 will soon begin to yield positive results in every nation. Drastic changes will manifest in the mentality, attitude and lifestyle of the people as they would have been nurtured in noble values that would ultimately result in unprecedented national growth and development.

CHAPTER ELEVEN

THE MEDIA AS ADVOCATES OF NATIONAL VALUES

T he pervasive power of the media in deciding, influencing and shaping people's perceptions and behaviors has been well-documented over the years. Media scholars and sociological researchers have found that the influence and reach of mass media is incalculable and universal. Everyone is exposed to mass media influence and it affects how we feel about everything, including products, people, events, and even ourselves.

One of the most popular theories that explain this power of the media is the hypodermic needle (or magic bullet) theory, which implies that the media have a direct, immediate and powerful effect on their audiences. The theory suggests that the media could influence a very large group of people directly and uniformly by 'shooting' or 'injecting' them with appropriate messages designed to trigger a desired response.

This theory suggests, for example, that a direct correlation exists between the violence and anti-social behavior portrayed in films, on television, in computer games, in rap lyrics, etc. and the violence and antisocial behavior such as drug use and teenage gun/knife crime found in real life. The theory further suggests that children and teenagers, in particular, are vulnerable to media content because they are still in the early stages of socialization and therefore very impressionable.

Events during the Second World War contributed significantly to the evolution of the hypodermic needle theory. The media then played a vital role in the way Nazi Germany successfully influenced the minds of Germans before and during the war. The German Nazi party, led by Adolf Hitler, developed extremely successful propaganda campaigns using simple slogans and images repeated over and again in order to win public support for the party. The Nazis spent huge sums on newspapers, leaflets and poster campaigns; they produced lots of movies about their objectives and achievements which made a great impact on Germans' minds.

The point I am trying to show you here is the power that the media wield on people's mentalities, opinions and attitudes. The media, in this context, encompasses radio, television, newspapers, magazines, music, movies and the Internet. I strongly agree with the view that the mass media have so much power in influencing people's decisions, as many individuals spend a significant part of their day consuming contents from the various media channels.

To this end, media owners, regulators and policy-makers have a great role to play in helping to instill the values and ideals of a nation in its citizens. In fact, as I will be showing you, much of the erosion that is sometimes observed in national values is traceable to the influence of certain media contents.

SPECIFIC MEDIA ROLES IN INCULCATING NATIONAL VALUES

1. Watchdogs of the Society

This is not just a traditional role of the media but a constitutional one as well. The media in most democracies, in particular, are seen as the "fourth estate of the realm" – coming after the executive, the legislative and the judicial arms of government. Interestingly, their role here is not an extension of the other three arms but an assessor of their performance in accordance with the constitution and the expectations of the electorates.

Essentially, the media serve to checkmate the excesses of the other arms of government to prevent abuses. They help in promoting ethics of public life by monitoring the conduct of government officials. And, as I mentioned before, this role is enshrined in the constitution of every democratic government of the world. For instance, Section 22 of the Nigerian 1999 constitution provides that: "the press, radio, television and other agencies of mass media shall at all times be free to uphold the fundamental objectives contained in this chapter and uphold the responsibility and accountability of the government to the people."

The question is, how much have the Nigerian media employed this mandate in promoting national values of honesty, integrity, transparency and accountability in public service? This, I must say, is crucial to motivating citizens to embrace and promote national values. When citizens observe that their leaders take national values seriously, it becomes easy for them to emulate them.

Moreover, I think there is a vital truth that the media must realize and which should galvanize them to really intensify their role as watchdogs. It was Lord Acton, English historian and politician, who wrote in April 1887 that "power tends to corrupt, and absolute power corrupts absolutely."1 Public office is not one that everyone has access to; thus, there is always the tendency for those who are elected or appointed into such position to begin to consider themselves above the laws and ethics of the society, rather being custodians of such. It is with this understanding that the constitution strategically empowers the media to curb such inimical tendency.

Unfortunately, the media have many times failed in this regards. Because of the allure of subventions, advert patronage and some other favors from public office holders, many media houses have made themselves lapdogs, rather than watchdogs. This way, public office holders are able to flagrantly circumvent laws and exhibit behaviors that contradict national values. Who will call such officials to account when the watchmen themselves have been converted to henchmen?

Only recently in Nigeria, the national anti-corruption agency, EFCC, disclosed that several media houses benefitted from funds that were supposed to be used to purchase arms to fight insurgency but allegedly diverted by the then National Security Adviser. How would these media outfits have been able to hold such official to accountability? The real downside of this laxity in duty by the media is that, as public officials are allowed to violate national values and the media even sometimes commend them, the impression that the majority of the citizens get is that these wrong patterns of behavior are acceptable, and thus national values become the casualty.

Closely related to the watchdog role is the surveillance role of the media which extends beyond the government to every segment of the entire society – individuals, institutions, groups, companies, agencies and so on. The media can play a significant role in promoting national values by beaming their searchlight on the society and reporting on people, practices and policies that are capable of either promoting or undermining the values of a nation. The media are not to be simply interested in sensational news, celebrity gossips or press releases from companies; it is their role to use their vantage position to project good behaviors, commend right practices, denounce wrong ones and generally ensure that the nation is constantly abiding by its national values.

2. Agenda-setting

By virtue of the power they wield upon the populace, the media can set national values as a dominant subject of thinking and discussion in a nation. This is achieved by the priority given to issues bordering on national values and the frequency with which they are reported.

Indeed, in this regard, the media appear to me to be the most potent agency of instilling national values. The point is that many people depend on the media in determining what issues form the heartbeat of a nation at every given point in time. When people pick up a newspaper or magazine, they are mostly interested in stories and headlines that have been given prominence by the media outlet. This is one of the special privileges the media have. The issues given prominence in newspapers and on television and radio talk shows, commentaries and phone-in programs may not necessarily be the most important events that are happening in a nation, but because the media give such issues special attention, everybody begins to talk about them.

You can then imagine what happens if the media decide to give special attention to the significance of national values, giving them prominence in news reports, editorials, commentaries, discussions and so on. It becomes something citizens begin to take seriously.

3. Advocacy

The media are in a very good position to initiate sustained

campaigns towards particular forms of behavior and attitudes. In the past, the media have been used in successful health campaigns. Just recently, Nigeria was commended for the swift efforts in combating and conquering the Ebola Virus Disease, which wreaked untold havocs on many other African countries. However, one of the truths that were established from that episode is the power of the media in influencing people's behavior.

For instance, over the years, not many Nigerians believed in regular hand-washing as a way of preventing illness. However, with the outbreak of Ebola, and the media disseminating the advice by health experts that regular hand-washing was a way of protecting oneself against the disease, the practice of hand-washing suddenly became a part of the daily life of Nigerians. The change was so drastic and incredible. Water dispensers and hand disinfectants suddenly became popular – from banks, to schools, to religious houses, to individual homes. Nigerians became so conscious of this aspect of hygiene overnight.

Of course, with the successful defeat of Ebola and consequent silence of the media on the issue of hygiene, not many people bother about such things anymore. But the reality is that if this same approach adopted by the media in tackling Ebola is employed in arresting erosion of national values, the extent of success can only be imagined. And unlike the case with the Ebola campaign, if the media decide to hold sustained campaigns and enlightenment on different aspects of national ethics – including patriotism, honesty, dignity of labor, integrity, truthfulness, loyalty, decency – the impact will reverberate throughout the nation.

Recently, the Nigerian government started intensifying efforts on making the citizens patronize made-in-Nigeria products. This is obviously due to the fact that many Nigerians have a penchant for disparaging anything local and patronizing everything foreign. The effects of these have been predictably destructive to the economy of the nation and the morale of entrepreneurs. I believe this is why the government has embarked on this campaign. But I'm not sure the government can achieve so much on this without the media acting as amplifiers of the message. Through repeated editorials, commentaries, analyses, discussions, drama pieces and documentaries, Nigerians must be taught to take pride in things that pertain to their nation.

4. Censoring programs/entertainment contents

I am giving particular attention to this point because one of the dominant ways in which values are either preserved or destroyed in a nation is the kind of contents featured in the media. And this especially concerns entertainment programs, comprising movies, music and other forms of entertainment.

It is really a matter of serious concern today that many countries, especially the developing ones, consider their cultures, values and customs to be inferior to those of developing nations. Many citizens of Nigeria, for example, believe that they are not enlightened or refined until they imbibe the totality of the customs and practices of people in Western nations. This is why there seems to be a cyclone of Western beliefs and practices sweeping through the entire nation, from the cosmopolitan cities to the most secluded villages. The most disturbing part is that, most times, it is often the illicit aspects of these foreign cultures that are imbibed and replicated.

Interestingly, most of the people who indulge in these foreign fantasies have never been outside the shores of their villages, much less country. So, who feeds them with the junk that poisons whatever values that they previously had? The media. How is this achieved? Through music and movies.

Unfortunately, the messages disseminated through these entertainment avenues, especially Hollywood products (and lately

Mexican telenovellas), are messages that glorify materialism, vanity, violence and immorality. Most of Nigeria's broadcast media outlets currently seem to be competing over which can broadcast the highest number of foreign programs, including sporting programs. The repercussion is that citizens become more familiar with the repeated contents and messages of theses program than the values and ideals of their own nation. Is it any wonder that indecency and delinquency rates are soaring among Nigerian youths, while national values are becoming alien and worthless?

But I don't think foreign music and movies are doing as much damage to national values as those currently being produced locally in Nigeria and many other African countries. Decades ago, local music and movies were basically for inculcating moral and national values. Nowadays, it's all a cacophony of obscenities. Many musicians and movie producers in these countries seem to have totally gone berserk in not just blindly copying the immoralities and indecencies they observe in their foreign counterparts but in actually trying to outdo them.

All you see these days are movies and music promoting lawlessness, witchcraft, fraud, drunkenness, infidelity, pride, arrogance and laziness – behaviors that totally negate national values. Yet the media present these behaviors as normal and everyone – young and old – is allowed to watch them at any time of the day. This is a trend that must be reversed for the media to be instrumental to instilling national values in the citizenry.

Of course the argument is always that the media are simply offering members of the society what they want. But what this shows is that the media are either ignorant of their expected role in nation-building or they are merely trying to cover up their inordinate quest to get patronage, popularity and advert revenues. This, of course, reflects the same aspect of corruption that has pervaded the society – seeking wealth by foul means.

The media are not meant to be conformists but reformists. As I have shown above, they have the power to influence people's thinking and behavior. So, rather than simply "going with the flow" and helping to further plunge national values deeper into the cesspool of evil and decadence, why can't they choose instead to help preserve and promote good values and redirect citizens towards the path of rectitude?

And this is where I must bring in the regulatory boards of the media and the entertainment industries. I am usually perturbed when I openly hear songs or stumble on videos promoting violence, womanizing, drug dealing, corruption and the likes on Nigerian media stations and the agencies empowered to regulate such output seem totally unconcerned.

These agencies and the media houses themselves need to wake up to the enormity of their responsibility as custodians of national values and ethics. There is a lot depending on them in ensuring that only media contents that promote good ethics and national values are featured in their outlets. And if they can consistently play their roles with utmost sense of patriotism, the current slide in commitment to national values will be stemmed and citizens will be roused to the usefulness of national values!

CHAPTER TWELVE

RELIGIOUS ORGANIZATIONS AS POWERFUL FORCES FOR INCULCATION OF NATIONAL VALUES AND IDEALS

There is no denying the mighty and manifold influence that religious leaders have over their followers. In fact, in many places, religious people tend to respect and respond to the dictates of their spiritual leaders than those of their governments. Many acts, noble and ignoble, have been dutifully carried out by individuals supposedly acting under the instruction of some religious leader. This is why a chapter such as this cannot be ignored in discussing strategies for instilling national values in the citizenry.

Especially in places like Africa and the Middle East, where religion is an integral part of the people's thinking and daily lives, any attempt at influencing and shaping people's attitudes, without consideration for the role of religious leaders, may end up in futility. Let me give you an example.

In 1998, the global polio eradication campaign (a joint effort of the World Health Organization, UNICEF, and the Rotary Foundation) was launched, with the target of ending polio by the year 2000. What emboldened the initiators of the campaign to give it such a short deadline was that a similar initiative had achieved remarkable success in the Americas. Actually, by 1994, polio was officially declared eliminated in all the Americas.

As at the time the global campaign was launched, Nigeria was one of the countries with the highest number of polio cases. And so anyone would have thought that the initiative would naturally be welcomed with gratitude. Surprisingly, however, when the campaign started, rumors began to be spread by some Islamic leaders that the vaccine was part of a western plot to sterilize Nigerians and that the vaccines were tainted. These preachers warned their followers not to have their children vaccinated against polio.

Naturally, this opposition resulted in a setback for attempts to eradicate the disease. In fact, so strong was the opposition that the campaign had to be brought to a temporary halt. But it wasn't even just polio vaccine the clerics were against; they also warned their followers not to take the measles vaccine.

The result of all this was that polio cases in Nigeria soared and spread to at least 20 other countries. And within the first three months of 2005, the country suffered 20,000 measles cases and 600 deaths. Of course, indigenes in the affected areas of Nigeria were not bothered about these repercussions. They seemed much more concerned about the consequences of disobeying their leaders than any other consideration.

Realizing their error, sponsors of the polio campaign had to redesign their strategy to include a pivotal aspect they had once ignored. According to Katherine Marshall of the Berkeley Centre for Religion, Peace and World Affairs, "From top to bottom, religious leaders were brought into the campaign. Information was a first critical step. Health officials met religious leaders and listened to their concerns. They explained the campaign and how the vaccine worked, including safeguards. Religious leaders visited countries which had successful campaigns and where the vaccine was manufactured. The political Organization of the Islamic Conference was brought into the act and helped in getting fatwas from respected Muslim scholars (especially from other African countries) that highlighted parents' responsibilities to vaccinate their children. So ending the de facto boycott of the polio campaign was not sufficient. Real success came only when religious leaders became actively involved in helping to organize and support the campaigns. As the program evolved, skeptics became advocates. Leaders had their own children vaccinated in public. The program was back on track…"[1]

That shows clearly how crucial religious leaders and organizations can be to the success of developmental and transformational programs. However, having established this fact, there is another major issue that has baffled many people for so long. Why is it that many of the countries that are ranked as the most corrupt in the world are also among the most religious?

Let me narrow my query down to Nigeria as a case study. Nigeria, as statistics have shown, is one of the most deeply religious countries. The country is divided between mainly Muslims in the north and predominantly Christians in the South. Almost on every street in Nigeria, there is a place of worship. On Fridays, some roads are blocked and mosques are filled as Muslims have their major religious observance. On Sundays, churches are besieged by Christians claiming to worship God in all sorts of ways. So, why is this country known to be so corrupt; or as the immediate past Prime Minister of Britain, David Cameron, recently described it, "fantastically corrupt"?

Again, I don't know if this has bothered you, as it has often bothered me: Many of the individuals that have been found guilty of criminal acts in Nigeria, whether as government officials, people in the corporate world or just as ordinary citizens, have one religion or the other which they practiced and some are even known to have been affiliated to some specific religious houses. So, what could be wrong? Why couldn't their attachment to religion prevent them from exhibiting a perverted value system?

I think the answer, from the polio example I cited above, is clear enough: Most of the religious houses and leaders only use the influence they have over their followers in very dubious ways that encourage behaviors and practices that threaten national values, rather than promote them. This is why you will see that despite the religiosity of Nigerians, many still engage in shady practices that are plunging the nation deeper into the abyss of corruption.

First of all, there are many occasions when religious leaders openly endorse corrupt individuals and urge their members to vote them into power, either simply on the basis of religious affiliation or because such corrupt individuals have donated huge sums of money or some other gratifications to the place of worship. This sends the wrong message to the followers.

According to Professor Badmus, Dean of Postgraduate School, University of Ilorin (UNILORIN), Nigeria, "religious leaders have not helped matters. They know the source of corruption. If corrupt people are coming with gifts and our religious leaders can be courageous to reject them, this will minimize corruption among the leaders we have in the society. So we appeal to our religious leaders to demonstrate courage and call a spade by its name and not to parry with the leaders that are devastating the people under them."[2]

Secondly, there are times when wealthy men and of questionable characters attend religious houses and they are given very special treatments, backed by endless encomiums, while the seemingly poor ones (despite being hardworking themselves) are practically disregarded. The message this sends to followers is that being wealthy is the fastest means of gaining respect and recognition before God – and they will be willing to go to any extent to achieve this wealth. Even the Bible frowns at such wealth-based preferential treatment. **"My brethren, do not hold the faith of our Lord Jesus Christ, the Lord of glory, with partiality. For if there should come into your assembly a man with gold rings, in fine apparel, and there should also come in a poor man in filthy clothes, and you pay attention to the one wearing the fine clothes and say to him, "You sit here in a good place," and say to the poor man, "You stand there," or, "Sit here at my footstool," have you not shown partiality among yourselves, and become judges with evil thoughts?"** (James 2:1-4).

Thirdly and most importantly, it is a known fact that in religious societies, their value system is naturally influenced by faith and religion. Thus, if the religious leaders themselves - who are supposed to be custodians of good values - practice, condone or celebrate corrupt practices, the message is quickly imbibed by the followers and automatically gets dispersed in the society. This is especially so today as the message of instant prosperity as a proof of God's presence has dominated the teachings in most religious houses.

Let me give you an example of this. A pastor could get to the pulpit on a Sunday in November or even December and say that somebody would be a millionaire before the end of the year. There might be up to 500 people in that auditorium and all of them would shout "amen!" Indeed, this kind of scenario happens often and you don't find the pastors clarifying things to their members that only people who work diligently and honestly, with firm faith in God, can have such miracles.

When pastors don't make such clarifications, everybody begins to believe that some magical miracles would happen. So, when someone in the congregation goes to his office and sees an unsigned check for a million dollars and nobody is claiming responsibility for it, he claims it. He believes that it is God that has provided it for him.

That is how corruption gets from the pulpit to the society. That particular member would claim that God has answered his pastor's prayer. He would boldly come to give testimony the following Sunday while the naïve and ignorant members would shout hallelujah! Meanwhile they too are expecting similar miracles and on and on. That is how the vicious cycle of corruption from the pulpit to the whole country runs.

Another value challenge in Nigeria that is especially contributed by the church is that church leaders often teach their millions of followers to expect miracles without telling them the truth about the order of life. People are not supposed to live with the mentality that they must daily depend on miracles to live a meaningful life; rather, we are supposed to live by the natural laws and principles that God has instituted to ensure order and balance in life.

This is why it is so common that no matter what you talk to a Nigerian about, he would simply tell you that God will do it. Nigerians are good at asking God to do for them what He expects them to do for themselves. Truth is, there is no way God can do for man, what he is supposed to do for himself. There is no way man can do for God what God can only do. This is why I think that most of the prayers in Nigeria (maybe about 80 percent) are a waste of time. This is because people continue to ask God to do what He has already done or what He has given them the ability to do for themselves.

Due to deceptive religious teachings, many Nigerians expect miracles from morning till night. This is why any opportunity that presents itself, godly or ungodly, they take it as God's miracle or blessing. This is how national values are disparaged and corruption is encouraged.

WHAT SHOULD RELIGIOUS LEADERS BE DOING?

Let me make something clear to you. The fact that I mentioned hard work and honesty as the primary gateways to true financial prosperity does not mean that I do not believe in divine breakthrough or miracles. As a pastor myself, I believe in breakthrough. But we religious leaders have to lay more emphasis on the values of hard work, dignity of labor, integrity, patience, perseverance and humility as prerequisites for having and sustaining wealth.

Actually, the word "breakthrough" is a word from "breaking forth". Water, springs or streams break forth from under the ground. Now note this: For water to break forth, it must have been forcing its way for ages or for years before it suddenly breaks through. This means that the breakthrough that we see all of a sudden is as a result of hard work, real hard work. Sadly, this is not often emphasized in religious houses. Preachers don't speak much on the value of hard work or preparation for success in life. They only emphasize the breakthrough part.

Another thing I think religious leaders should be emphasizing more is that it is wrong to think that the only way to succeed and prosper in life is to depend on prayers. That is another root of corruption. When people have such mindset, it easily turns them to religious gamblers and fraudsters. Everybody goes out of a prayer center and starts looking for automatic wealth and prosperity. Consequently, any opportunity they see, even if illegal, they want to take advantage of.

People must be taught that the possibility of miracle is not the order of the day. It is only two percent of our daily life that should depend on miracles from God. The order of life is strict adherence to God's laws and principles. It is obedience to the laws of God that brings wealth and blessings.

Religious leaders must emphasize it to their followers that the rule of life is that you work hard for your results. You don't wait for grace or favor to give you results without working for them. They must declare that, if you don't work for wealth, even if you get that wealth through your parents, relatives or spouse, you are still a thief (see Proverbs 28:24). You are robbing the people who gave you that wealth.

Christian religious leaders, in particular, must desist from teaching people to claim everything "by faith". When you teach that people can claim anything, how can they claim when they are not qualified for it? How can they just claim simply because they have greed for it? This is a way of promoting greed, covetousness and lust in the society.

There is no product without the process of production. So, it is wrong to tell people that they can get anything they want by demonstrating faith or "sowing seeds" through tithes and offerings. Not that I don't believe in tithe and offering but that is not the way of receiving wealth. It is the way of preventing curses from coming to your resources.

Pastors must teach their members that for you to really have wealth, giving tithes and offerings is not enough. Tithes and offerings open up heaven to you. God doesn't send money from heaven. You have to go to work and be involved in the process of production. It is only that way that wealth and riches will come to you.

In summary therefore, a major way that religious leaders can help instill national values is to desist from promoting the culture of getting something for nothing; it is to stop promoting the culture of frivolity, vanity and ostentation. It is to stop promoting the belief that anyone who is not wealthy is abnormal, inferior or out of favor with God. It is to encourage their followers to always demonstrate their faith through the values of diligence, creativity, truthfulness, honesty and perseverance!

CHAPTER THIRTEEN

PRESSURE GROUPS AND CIVIL SOCIETIES AS WATCHDOGS FOR THE VALUES AND IDEALS OF A NATION

D uring the recent Second Annual Lecture of the Lagos State University School of Communications held in July 2016, President of the African Public Relations Association (APRA), Mr. Yomi Badejo-Okusanya, made this striking remark:

"The Federal Government's on-going fight against corruption stands the risk of being totally dissipated if **concise and strategic effort** *is not made to drive change in the mindset of the today's Nigerian youth. Unfortunately, an alarming number of them are not bothered about the negatives of being involved in corruption as long as they are not caught in the act, laying the ground for a mortgaged future."1*

Badejo-Okusanya was saying this, partly in commendation of the effort of the Buhari-led administration in waging war against corruption in Nigeria, and partly to stress the need to broaden the strategies being employed in the campaign. In his own estimation, while the punitive measures currently being employed against those guilty of corruption are laudable, they must also be accompanied by virile advocacy that appeals to human reasoning, showing the devastating effects of corruption.

The question that immediately follows such an interesting and enlightening recommendation is: Who is in the best position to implement the orientation and advocacy needed to disseminate the message on the evils of corruption and gains of dignity of labor? Some may say it's the work of the National Orientation Agency, the orientation arm of the Federal Government of Nigeria. However, as history and research have shown, the task of national orientation on values cannot be left to the government alone. When that happens, as has been seen in countries like Nigeria, very little can be achieved.

To drive home the messages of responsibility, accountability, patriotism, honesty, dignity of labor and other components of the value system of a nation, other well-meaning individuals and groups must rise to the challenge of propagating national values, engaging in advocacy and lobbying for policies and practices that will foster advancement of national heritage and values. These must constitute themselves into watchdogs against erosion and perversion of national ideals.

I have mentioned the roles of the school system, the media and religious organizations in helping to achieve this. However, I must point out that equally pivotal to success in orientation of citizens and waging war against corruption of national values is the role of pressure groups.

Pressure groups, in the course of history, have played and continue to play an important part in the development of political and social systems. As their name implies, they are groups that are formed for the purpose of exerting pressure on government and policy-makers in order to protect or advance a particular cause or interest.

Pressure groups have been defined as voluntary associations of individuals who band together for the defense of a particular interest. Interest in this sense is a conscious desire to have a public policy or the authoritative allocation of values, and to move in a particular, general or specific direction.

Examples of pressure groups in Nigeria include: The Nigerian Labour Congress (NLC), which promotes the rights, well-being and the interests of all workers, pensioners and the trade unions in Nigeria; Socio-Economic Rights & Accountability Project (SERAP), which serves to promote transparency and accountability in the public and private sectors through human rights; National Association of Nigerian Students (NANS), which serves the interests of Nigerian students in higher institutions of learning; Arewa Consultative Forum (ACF), which is arguably the most influential group in Northern Nigeria; Oanaeze Ndigbo, which is involved in matters affecting the interest and general welfare of the Igbos in Nigeria and the rest of the world; Afenifere, which is a socio-cultural organization formed to advance the interest of the Yoruba people; Ijaw Youth Council (IYC), which is the most active pressure group in the South South region of Nigeria; the Christian Association of Nigeria (CAN), which is an association of Christian churches in Nigeria; The Nigerian Supreme Council for Islamic Affairs (NSCIA) which advances the interests of Islam and the Muslims throughout Nigeria, and so on.

Let me say here that even though the common perception of pressure groups (also known as advocacy groups, lobby groups, campaign groups, interest groups, or special interest groups) is that their activities are directed primarily at the government; in reality, their role is much more comprehensive than serving as a channel through which citizens express their opinion in a political system.

It comprises using various forms of advocacy in order to influence both public policy and public opinion. This means that pressure groups can serve both as instruments of defending their primary interests and the masses, as well as playing the role of educating, sensitizing and mobilizing the same masses towards particular courses of action that are not necessarily aimed at influencing the government but at bringing behavioral and attitudinal changes in them.

To explain this further, let me highlight the three major roles of pressure groups and what they should be doing, within the context of inculcating, promoting and preserving national values.

1. Facilitating laws and policies that will ensure responsible leadership and followership

Here is a simple truth. The reasons some particular crimes and vices thrive in certain countries and communities is because there are no solid legislations that will act as deterrents to the citizens. Let me give you an example. Within the past few years, when the ISIS terrorist group began to gain notoriety for its atrocities, many European citizens left their countries to join the group. You know why? Some people say it's a result of radicalization. This is partly true, but there is certainly more to it.

As research and experience have shown, one of the factors encouraging people to join the group is that many of these ISIS converts know that regardless of the depravity of their actions, they would still retain their citizenship and could therefore still return freely to their native countries whenever they like. Suppose there was a legislation that says that joining the group is tantamount to renouncing your citizenship (which should actually be the case) the mad rush to join the murderous group would have been significantly curtailed.

The same applies to countries like the US and the UK, where the rates of drug addiction, slothfulness, drunkenness and teenage pregnancy are astronomical. Check if there are legislations that can deter such objectionable tendencies and you would be shocked to find that what they have instead are provisions that would further encourage people that are involved in such behaviors.

The case of the UK is particularly worrisome. Decades of handing out special benefits to the unemployed and the disabled have produced generations of citizens who are not just without gainful employment but have actually sworn never to work. After all, what is the point of working when you can enjoy almost all the benefits that a gainfully employed person gets? It's the same sad story with teenage pregnancy. A pregnant teenage British citizen knows that she is automatically entitled to free housing and other benefits. How is this going to deter promiscuity or teenage pregnancy? Pressure groups can do a lot in making the government know the cumulative dangers of such indulgences.

Now, let me come to Nigeria. Why is corruption so common and criminal activities so rampant in Nigeria? Why are vices such as examination malpractice, bribery and Internet scam so pervasive? Don't look elsewhere for the answers. It is because of either absence of legislation or weakness in enforcement. Why is drug trafficking rife in a place like Nigeria but rare in a place like Indonesia? You can easily guess the answer. In Indonesia, you stand the risk of capital punishment if convicted, while in Nigeria, the maximum sentence (which is never applied anyway) is 15 years imprisonment. This is why no month passes by without news of persons being caught trying to smuggle hard drugs in or out of the country, using different means. Even some who claim to be going on pilgrimage to Holy Lands cannot resist the allure of smuggling drugs because the potential rewards far outweigh the potential risks.

Irked by this trend, a Nigerian newspaper wrote in its editorial a few years back: "We are concerned at the alarming rate at which Nigerians continue to engage in illicit drug trafficking, despite measures taken by the NDLEA to dissuade them from the illegal act. The drug traffickers continue to get desperate and invent novel methods of carrying out their lawless act. It is our opinion that many Nigerians continue to traffic in drugs because the punishment for the offence is not harsh enough. They continue to engage in it because they feel the benefits far outweigh the risks. This is why we are calling on the Federal Government to revisit the penalty for drug trafficking in the country and make it more severe. If a would-be drug trafficker knew that the risks far outweigh the benefits, he or she would think twice before engaging in the illicit trade."2

But the truth is that such calls by the media won't achieve much without being backed by serious actions, which only pressure groups can catalyze. Pressure groups in the country must go beyond personal interests and think of national interests. They must think of how to leverage their power to influence enactment of laws and initiation of policies that will engender and ensure that both the leadership and the citizens shun corrupt practices. Many politicians in the country compete in ostentatious display of their ill-gotten wealth with impunity. The reason is because they know they can get away with such flamboyance very easily. Even for people who have obtained their wealth through seemingly legal means, the rate of vain extravagance that has apparently become a normal way of life wouldn't be so, if tax laws were taken seriously. This, again, is a key area where pressure groups can come to the rescue.

Pressure groups can perform this role of influencing laws and policies that will help in curbing corruption and indiscipline in two ways - directly and indirectly. In the direct sense, pressure groups can engage in lobbying the government, writing open letters and advertorials, sponsoring bills and conducting public opinion polls – the results of which will be published for the government to know what steps to take. And when these seem ineffective, peaceful protests can be carried out to let the government know what it should be doing.

In the indirect sense, pressure groups can rouse the citizens and enlist their support in getting the government to do the needful. Historically, pressure groups have proven to be powerful in mobilizing people towards making momentous demands from their governments. Most of the revolutions and reforms in history have been triggered by the relentless mobilization and rallying of the masses. In Nigeria, pressure groups such as NADECO were enormously influential during the military era. And in the current fourth republic, one cannot forget easily the roles of groups such as the Save Nigeria Group in mobilizing the masses to influence government policies. I believe that, more than ever before, a lot more work needs to be done in this regard.

2. Being watchdogs against corrupt practices and pursuing criminal cases till justice is done

One area in which the Nigeria media have not been doing well enough in instilling national values is the aspect of following through on reported criminal cases until successful prosecution is secured. Almost every day, there are reports of criminal activities from different part of the country, but it seems that the media mostly stop at reporting and unlike most of their counterparts in developed countries, they do not follow up on such cases.

However, to be fair to them, I think the main problem actually lies with the docility of Nigerians and the apathy of pressure groups towards such cases. Naturally, in a country where national values are considered very important, when cases of fraud and corruption in high places are reported and are seen to be getting rampant, pressure groups take the case up from there and begin to mount pressure on the government to take concrete steps to ensure that the cases are duly investigated. And when anyone is found guilty, they ensure that appropriate punishments are meted as a form of deterrent.

Pressure groups can be so influential that when judges hand down ridiculous judgments to criminals (either because of an error or due to deliberate perversion of justice), they go all out to register their concerns and they rouse the consciousness of the citizens to such travesty. Even if the judge does not reverse the judgment, the awareness created would make other judges to be more thorough and conscientious in their duty.

However, pressure groups in Nigeria have been quite disappointing in this area in recent times. In fact, rather than being watchdogs against corruption, some have actually turned themselves to enemies of justice and anti-corruption campaigns. Recently, some pressure groups in the Southern region, which originally claimed to be fighting for the interest of the well-being of the region (especially the environment) have been threatening to cause mayhem if some top leaders from the region who were in the last administration are tried for corruption.

Except for SERAP, which has been making some commendable efforts, most pressure groups currently in Nigeria seem to be in a state of perpetual sedation as far as cases of corruption and successful investigation and prosecution are concerned. Let me cite a few particularly baffling instances.

In 2012, a committee was set up to look into subsidy scam allegedly perpetrated by some oil companies in the country. In the wake of the investigations, reports surfaced that the chairman of the committee demanded for bribes running into hundreds of millions of dollars from one oil mogul, whose company was one of those indicted. Reportedly, there were even video and audio evidences to back up the bribery claim. The accused chairman denied the allegations and claimed that it was actually the mogul who was mounting pressure on him to take bribe, which he eventually took to implicate the mogul.

Now, the baffling thing is that to date, nothing significant has come out of this scandal. Even worse is that the committee chairman, who was a lawmaker as at the time the scandal broke, continued with his legislative duties till the end of his tenure. One can only wonder – where were the pressure groups in the country at this time?

In 2014, the Nigerian Immigration Service (NIS) advertised for job applications into 4000 vacant positions. The agency collected an application fee from the applicants and about 6.5 million job-seekers from all over the nation were invited to various centers to take recruitment test the same day. Obviously, there was no way the few centers selected for the test (six in all) could have the capacity for such large number of people. Consequently, in all of the centers, as the applicants jostled for space and the organizers struggled in vain to control the crowd, accidents of all sorts occurred, leaving at least 16 young men and women dead and several others injured. Shockingly, the then Minister of Internal Affairs, who had the control of the NIS retained his job and instead tried to pass the blame to others. Pressure groups remained mute and the families of the deceased were left to suffer in silence.

As I write now, the principal officers of the two houses of parliament in Nigeria are embroiled in alleged scandals bordering on forgery, fraud and false declaration of assets. But rather than step aside for independent investigation to be carried out, as it is done in other respectable countries, these principal leaders continue in their positions - making laws for the citizens, while cases of lawlessness hang on them. And you wonder whether pressure groups are in such a country!

Several similar cases as the above are daily overlooked in Nigeria. And this accounts for why the value system of the country is so bastardized. To the young generation and other observers, the silence of these pressure groups and other relevant groups in the country is a sign that such aberrant behaviors are normal and the result is that they are emulated and replicated. This is why I continue to advocate that pressure groups in Nigeria really need to wake up from their detrimental slumber.

3. Enlightening and re-orientating citizens toward attitudinal and behavioral change

I consider this as the most important function that pressure groups should be performing, especially in countries like Nigeria. Unfortunately as I noted before, most pressure group activities these days are either targeted at promoting self-interest or targeted at criticizing the government on behalf of the citizens. But beyond these activities, however, is the need to turn the citizens towards themselves, to make them reflect individually, rather than pointing fingers at the government for all the wrongs in the society.

Citizens have to be made to know, through strategic and spirited campaigns, that there is a lot they can do themselves to ensure a peaceful, progressive and prosperous society. They must be encouraged to support government's anti-corruption efforts. They must be made to know that there is much they can do improve the image of the country to foreigners, especially through the way they conduct themselves at airports and in foreign countries.

I'm really appalled when I find some pressure groups trying to compel the government to plead on behalf of Nigerians in overseas prisons, especially those on death row. I don't think pressure groups should only be waking up when crimes have been committed and appropriate sentences have been passed. I think the right time to speak up is before citizens get themselves involved in criminal acts. Intensive and repeated orientation programs must be organized, especially for citizens traveling overseas on the necessity of abiding with the laws of their host countries. They should be warned that no one will plead for them should they go ahead to willfully violate such laws.

What I'm saying in essence, is that citizens must be taught by pressure groups on the need for personal responsibility. A society does not change through some magical wand or miracle prayers; a society changes when individual citizens decide to change - when each citizen decides to change the way they do things in their individual circles.

Citizens must be made to know that they cannot be waiting for the government to correct all the ills in the society. They must be sensitized to be watchdogs of each other's behavior and be ready to denounce acts of corruption and indiscipline. Sometimes you find a citizen engaging in gross acts of indiscipline, such as defecating or urinating in public places; defacing public buildings with graffiti or posters; or vandalizing public properties - and no one bothers to correct them. The government can't see all of these things but the citizens can. So let the pressure groups get busy with this!

The Nigerian Labor Congress (NLC) for instance can organize seminars, workshops and other relevant programs on ethics for workers in general. NLC can't restrict itself to just fighting for workers' rights; it should be promoting workers' responsibilities as well. The National Association of Nigerian Students (NANS) can't just settle for just creating a hullabaloo or threatening chaos when any of its members is assumed to have been ill-treated by school authorities – it should equally be at the forefront of campaigning for diligence, decency and discipline among students.

Same goes for other pressure groups that are only concerned with narrow interests. Each should be involved in encouraging members to imbibe values of responsibility, honesty, hard work, truthfulness, tolerance and integrity. If each of the pressure groups in the country were to be actively involved in these enlightenment and sensitization activities, the country will definitely get better for all, and most of the parochial agitations may no longer be necessary.

4. Providing voice for the voiceless and safeguarding whistleblowers

This is one other important role that I think pressure groups, civil organizations and NGOs should be playing in a nation, especially with the intention of promoting national values. I mentioned it above that citizens should be encouraged to be watchdogs of aberrant and unpatriotic behaviors in the society and take appropriate actions of denouncing or reporting to appropriate authorities where necessary. But there have been cases where whistleblowers become victimized for speaking out the truth, and most times, they are left regretting their decisions to do the right.

I think pressure groups and relevant NGOs will do well to promote good values among citizens if they make potential whistleblowers know that they will be supported and shielded against victimization. It is because of this lack of assurance that many citizens keep quiet, while wrong practices go on around them.

There is an ongoing example of failure of Nigerian pressure groups in this regard. Recently, a member of the Federal House of Representatives raised the alarm that some prominent members of the House had been involved in fraudulent acts while assessing the country's budget. He also made startling allegations that members of the House had been allocating to themselves huge sums of money that could have been used for developmental projects in the country.

Now, whether the allegations are true or not is not my main concern here. My main concern has been the turn of events, following the series of weighty allegations made against the principal lawmakers. Since the startling revelations, rather than the police and the anti-corruption agencies in the country conducting an independent investigation, their focus has been on the whistleblower himself and several accusations have been leveled against him. Having been left untouched, the accused principal officers of the House became more emboldened and have gone ahead to suspend the whistleblower from his duties, while they continue holding their various positions.

In all these, the Nigerian populace seems totally unbothered and the pressure groups that one would expect to rouse the populace to the travesty going on among those making laws for the country are themselves apathetic. Looking at this appalling development, how many citizens would still want to expose criminal activities, knowing for sure that "the hunter" may end up being "the hunted"?

Pressure groups can also be helpful in cases where the rights of certain citizens are being trampled upon by those who consider themselves so wealthy, powerful or influential that they cannot be touched. When pressure groups encourage citizens who are victims of abuse to report to them for appropriate action and they fulfill their promise by taking reported cases up till justice is done, more cases of abuse will be reported and investigated, which will make those who had considered themselves untouchable to be wary in continuing in wrongdoing.

Of course, most of the roles I have listed here are similar to those prescribed for the media, but let me make it clear that these two groups can't perform these roles in the same way. Due to certain differences in their formation, structure and reach, there are differences in the ways these duties are carried out. Fortunately, the differences are quite complementary.

For instance, while the media have the advantage of quickly reaching a mass audience, they do not have the personal touch and the dynamism with which pressure groups can disseminate and pursue relevant cases. Moreover, the media can set agenda that will set pressure groups to action, while pressure groups can equally provide the media with credible information, statistics and opinion poll results that can be analyzed and used as news items for the government and the entire populace to be aware of happenings in the society.

It is my firm belief that, if all the various agencies and groups mentioned above, can individually and collectively play their roles, much more will be achieved in discouraging acts of corruption and encouraging citizens to imbibe, promote and preserve the values and ideals of the founding fathers of their nation. Citizens themselves will be agents of national transformation, rather than waiting for the imaginary magical wands of the government to bring about the much needed progress and development in all aspects of their national life.

CHAPTER FOURTEEN

THE FAMILY AS AN ENGRAVER AND PROMOTER OF NATIONAL VALUES

"Train up a child in the way he should go, And when he is old he will not depart from it" (Proverbs 22:6)

The role of the family as the first and most important agent of socialization – and thus, of inculcation of national values – cannot be overemphasized. The family is the most significant social institution and one with the most far-reaching impact on the moral and spiritual fabrics of the society. The reason for this is obvious. Everyone in the world comes through a certain family, and the nature, structure and culture of that family will go a long way in shaping the mentality and character of such individual. And more importantly, it will determine how the individual will perceive and react to the world around him.

The implication of this is that neither heroes nor villains suddenly drop from the sky and begin to transform or deform their society; they all spring from a source. Neither law-abiding citizens nor law-breakers are born that way; they are all products of certain kinds of socialization processes.

Interestingly, Psychologists and educationists have clearly established that every child born into the world has a blank mind, just like a blank slate (tabula rasa), which is waiting to be filled with something. It is what is engraved on this blank slate that influences the child's attitudes and actions throughout life. Beyond this, however, it has equally been established that the first five years of a child's life are critical for development. The experiences the child has in these early years help to determine the kind of adult he will become. Indeed it is extremely difficult for a child to unlearn whatever values, examples and behavioral traits he has imbibed within these "formative" years.

Biologists too have affirmed that within the first five years of life, a child's brain develops more and faster than at any other time in his life. Consequently, his early experiences within this period – the things he sees, hears, touches, smells and tastes – stimulate his brain, creating millions of connections. This is when the foundations for learning, health and behavior throughout life are laid down.

It is for this crucial reason that the Bible so assuredly declares that once a child has been properly trained the way he should go, he would not forget the training all through his life. Even Aristotle, the ancient Greek philosopher, once proclaimed, "Give me a child until he is seven and I will show you the man" – by which he meant that whatever way of thinking, acting and reacting that has been instilled in a child by age seven is a certain indicator of the kind of adult life the child would have and the role he will end up playing in society. As it is rightly said, "Old habits die hard!"

Fortunately, it is the family - the child's first point of contact with the society - that has the great responsibility and privilege of making the most of these early years of the child to mold him into a responsible member of the society. It is within the family that the child first learns to venerate or desecrate spiritual, moral and national values. Indeed, you can hardly find a biography or an autobiography of a national hero or villain in which no allusion is made to the contribution of the individual's upbringing to the role they ended up playing in their society. This confirms the assertion of William Goode that "it is within the family that the child is first socialized to serve the needs of the society and not only its own needs" (Goode, 1982).

BUILDING STRONG CHARACTER TRAITS

Now, having known the powerful and, I dare say, permanent role that the family consciously or unconsciously plays in helping to instill, uphold and promote national values, what should parents in particular be doing, to ensure that individuals passing through them to the society, become national assets and not liabilities? It begins with understanding and accepting their indispensable role in nation building, as well as realizing that the greatest gift they can give to their children is to help them become responsible to themselves, their families and their society. Armed with this knowledge, parent must then deliberately begin the process of building strong character traits in their children.

In its illuminating publication, *Helping Your Child Become a Responsible Citizen1*, the United States Department of Education defines "character" as "a set of qualities, or values, that shape our thoughts, actions, reactions and feelings." It goes further to outline the components of a strong character that must be inculcated in every child. These include:

- Compassion;
- Honesty and fairness;
- Self-discipline;
- Good judgment;

- Respect for others;
- Courage in upholding personal convictions;
- A strong sense of responsibility;
- Deep concern for the progress of one's community; and
- Maintaining self-respect at all times.

I will be explaining each of these elements shortly; but first let me point out the most important element of a strong character that is missing in the above list: FEAR OF GOD. This is the very foundation of a sound character that is needed to build up and advance a nation.

Now, let's consider the strategy for achieving this character building objective. Proverbs 22:6 which I quoted earlier gives us the principle for instilling unforgettable values in children. It says "TRAIN UP a child..."! I will be analyzing what this means by looking at the letters that make up the words TRAIN UP.

STRATEGY FOR RAISING NATION BUILDERS

T – Teaching

Parents must create time to consciously teach their children noble values and virtues that will empower them to be God-fearing individuals, exemplary citizens, change agents and nation builders. What parents teach their children on what is morally acceptable or not has the potential to stick to their minds and influence their behavior all through life. A classic example of this is found in the biblical story of the children of Johnadab, whose father's teaching so took root in them that not even a Prophet like Jeremiah could make them do something different from what they had been taught (see Jeremiah 35:2-11). In fact, by the time Jeremiah approached them, their father had long died, but his teachings continued to live on in them.

Now what should be the contents of the teaching? Let's

return to our components of a strong character. First is **fear of God**, which has to do with a deep reverence for the personality, commandments and supremacy of the Almighty God. Children must be made to know that everyone on earth is accountable to the immortal and invisible creator, who sees all we do in secret and in the open, and rewards everyone according to their deeds. This consciousness can serve as the most compelling motivation to choose a life of virtue above a life of vice. Next is **compassion**, which has to do with identifying with and being concerned about other people's needs. Children who are painstakingly taught compassion can never grow up to be bullies, abusers, fraudsters, extortionists, robbers, embezzlers or dictators because they have been molded to be sensitive to the needs of others. Next is **honesty and fairness**. Honesty has to do with truthfulness, trustworthiness and personal integrity. It involves presentation of facts as they are, rather than lying about them or exaggerating them. It means shunning every appearance of falsehood and deception, which form the basis of most of the corrupt practices we see in society today. It also has to do with admitting one's fault when one goes wrong, instead of trying to cover up or mislead others. Fairness has to do with handling situations based on facts and not bias, sentiments or prejudice. Teaching children this, helps them to grow up making upright decisions in dealing with others.

Next is **self-discipline** which has to do with delaying gratification, avoiding over-indulgence, controlling one's emotions, feelings and cravings. It also involves setting goals (for instance, preparing a time-table or "to-do" list) and sticking to it, proper use of time and learning to be patient. Next is **good judgment.** Children must be taught on making wise decisions in all situations and being able to discern between what is good and what is bad, what is right and what is wrong, what constitutes bravery and what is sheer recklessness and so on. Next is **respect for others**

– which means treating others the way one wishes to be treated. There is beauty in diversity. No one likes to be abused, belittled, ridiculed or discriminated against, for whatever reason. With this kind of teaching, children learn to appreciate and relate with others, regardless of differences in backgrounds, gender, social status, race, ethnicity or nationality. Respect for others also involves respect for constituted authorities, for leadership, government and national symbols and monuments. The significance of this must be explained to the child. Next is **self-respect** which means appreciating one's uniqueness and conducting oneself with dignity, decorum and decency at all times and in all places. This kind of teaching helps the child to grow to avoid anything that will destroy his reputation or bring shame to his family.

Next is **courage** in upholding one's convictions. This is quite essential as people generally (and youngsters in particular) are often desperate to have a sense of belonging. They don't want to be considered misfits and thus isolated. Sadly, this has been the foundation of many social ills, whether in schools, organizations or public service. As people say, "If you're in Rome, behave like the Romans"; or "If you can't beat them, join them." Children must be taught that it is better to stand alone in integrity than to be in a bad company. They must be taught it is better to stand up for who they are, rather than pretending to be who they're not. Next is **responsibility.** This means, first of all, taking responsibility for one's life and decisions, rather than blaming others. It means being diligent and believing in the dignity of honest labor. It also means being faithful to one's promises, honoring agreement with others and learning to be punctual. Next is **interest in communal progress**. This means, first of all, awareness and appreciation of the cultural values of their community and ancestry; as well as shunning self-centeredness and learning to sacrifice personal interest for the general good. Children who are brought up with this kind of mentality cannot be living in wealth while others around them languish in want. They are ever eager to contribute to the progress of others and their community.

Can you imagine what kind of society we would have if everyone imbibes the above values right from childhood? Where would people learn to be corrupt, lazy, unfaithful, immoral, decadent, violent and manipulative when these values have been properly inculcated in them? Can it not be rightly said then that the family bears the primary blame for the bulk of the corrupt practices that we observe in public service, government and the society in general?

Let me also emphasize that teaching children must be done both routinely (according to set times, in which parents create time to discuss with their children) as well as spontaneously, as the need arises.

R- Role-modeling

This is the most critical aspect of child training towards national development. It has the power to either consolidate every other element in the training process or totally frustrate the entire process altogether. The reason is simple. Children learn faster and better by what they see than what they hear. Every principle of character building as mentioned above will be of no effect in the life of a child if the family members – parents, in particular – do not model the principles themselves. In fact, it can be argued that the reason so many vices pervade the society today is not really because parents don't teach good morals (of course, I agree that many fail in this area as well) but because they don't practice what they teach.

Aesop, in one of his fables, tells an interesting story about a crab who once said to her child, "Daughter, why do you walk so one-sided? It is far more becoming to go straight forward." The young crab replied: "Quite true, dear mother; and if you will show me the straight way, I will promise to walk in it." Of course, the mother tried in vain to walk straight herself, and she had to finally agree that she was not in a good position to correct her child's lousy pattern of walking.

The point is, the apple doesn't fall far from the tree. Whatever parents wish to see in the lives of their children must be CONSISTENTLY demonstrated by themselves. Parents may spend all their lives preaching about compassion, honesty, respect for others, discipline, decency, decorum and whatnot. But if their children know them to be lazy, selfish, rude, violent, aggressive, abusive, using foul language, dishonest, insulting authorities, peeing in public places, boasting about skipping taxes, using false measures in business, engaging in shady transactions, dressing indecently, being unfaithful to promises, not contributing anything towards communal progress, jumping queues, flouting traffic rules, buying favors for their children in examination or other competitive engagements, for disobeying some other regulations, then the children cannot be expected to do better. Indeed, the children are likely to do worse! In Nigeria, currently, there are a number of politicians who are notorious for corruption and lawlessness. Unsurprisingly, some of them had parents who were once in public service and exhibited the same propensities.

A – Affirmation

Affirmation refers to words and acts of encouragement, appreciation and commendation towards children when they do what is right, especially using their initiative. As I mentioned earlier, children's minds need shaping towards the particular direction or orientation we want it to have. Even after teaching them, they may not be absolutely sure whether certain deeds are right or not. But as we express our approval or commendation for positive actions from them, it helps to consolidate their understanding of what is right and they will desire to take more of such actions until they become lifelong habits. Put simply, affirmation helps to program your child's mind into believing in his actions, as well as letting him know that it pays to do right. It also helps him to to recognize and build on his strengths, which would have become a solid part of him by the time he gets into adulthood.

I – Illustrations

Teaching, role-modeling and affirmations become much more effective when backed up with interesting stories and allusions that help to underscore our messages. Children are fascinated by story-telling because it helps for create vivid images in their minds which they not only fight delightful but also memorable. In teaching them values therefore, it will be effective to use factual or fictional stories of individuals (whether from the Bible, books and contemporary times) who carried out great acts of heroism, courage, patriotism, honesty, kindness etc. and were rewarded; as well as those of villains who indulged in acts of laziness, criminality and compromise and the punishments they got. This will further strengthen children's resolve to do what's right at all times.

N - Nurturing

Nurturing, apart from entailing provision of basic needs for children, also involves patiently and painstakingly coaching and observing them for practical demonstrations of the lessons and virtues that they have been taught. For instance, it is not enough to teach children about dignity of labor; we must give them chores and tasks to carry out within specific deadlines. It is not enough to teach them politeness; we must make them use expressions like "please", "thank you", "excuse me", "I'm sorry" etc when necessary. It is not enough to teach them compassion and selflessness; we must guide them to demonstrate such in practical ways towards their siblings and friends. In all of this, we must be patient and understanding as we help them grow into responsible adults. We must also guide them on choice of friendship, amusement, entertainment etc.

U - Upbraiding

Just as we create time to praise children when they do right, we must also correct and when necessary discipline them with love when they go wrong. This is a very critical part of raising responsible individuals and citizens. Many parents have ended up raising monsters and criminals for the society because they were afraid to discipline or upset their children. On the other hand, there are parents who wish to discipline their children but are handicapped by certain laws and psychological theories that have only ended up encouraging juvenile delinquencies in many nations of the world.

The strict injunction of the supreme word of God for raising responsible children is: **"Discipline your children while they are young enough to learn. If you don't, you are helping them destroy themselves."** (Proverbs 19:18, GNT). It is for the good of the family and the nation when parents are quick to observe traits of delinquencies in children and quickly nip such in the bud in love but with firmness. Children need to know that there are boundaries that must not be crossed. They need to know that they cannot always have their way in life. They need to know that rules and regulations must be obeyed. They need to know that there are repercussions for violations of natural, spiritual, moral and national laws.

P – Prayer

In all that families do to raise responsible children, constant prayers must not be neglected. Not only will praying for and with children help to make our training efforts effective but it also makes the children realize the importance of God in their daily lives and aspirations. Prayers provide parents with wisdom to train children aright, as well as guiding the children themselves in the path of uprightness, while shielding them from the corrupting influences in the society.

In addition to all that has been said concerning parents inculcating strong values in their children, I think that most importantly, it will help if the entire family can have established values that are upheld by every member at all times. This way, each member can be a "police" for the other member, when he or she seems to be deviating from these family values. Crimes and destruction of national values will drastically reduce in the society when each family member helps the other to do what's right at all times, rather than being accomplices in evil – as is so common today.

LAST NOTES

I am certain that you would agree with me that it has been a highly expository and enlightening journey so far in this book. We have had several revelations and made massive discoveries about nations in general. Specifically, I have shown you, with ample evidences from the Scriptures, scientific reports and historical accounts, that the formation, composition and positioning of nations are never by accident. God is the master planner and ultimate ruler of the universe and He has specific callings for each nation - callings that must be diligently ascertained and dutifully pursued for a nation to attain its maximum potential and justify the essence of its existence.

I have equally proved to you that most of the socio-political anomalies and catastrophes besetting many nations of the world today are direct repercussions of deviation from the original blueprint of God. Additionally, I have shown you the various agencies and strategies that could help nations to strengthen and safeguard their commitment to their callings.

The question now is, what is the point of all this? How should individuals, groups governments and nations react to these poignant revelations? Let me show you a classic template from the Scripture. 2 Kings 23:1-22 says:

"Now the king sent them to gather all the elders of Judah and Jerusalem to him. The king went up to the house of the Lord with all the men of Judah, and with him all the inhabitants of Jerusalem—the priests and the prophets and all the people, both small and great. And he read in their hearing all the words of the Book of the Covenant which had been found in the house of the Lord. Then the king stood by a pillar and made a covenant before the Lord, to follow the Lord and to keep His commandments and His testimonies and His statutes, with all his heart and all his soul, to perform the words of this covenant that were written in this book. And all the people took a stand for the covenant.

And the king commanded Hilkiah the high priest, the priests of the second order, and the doorkeepers, to bring out of the temple of the Lord all the articles that were made for Baal, for Asherah, and for all the host of heaven; and he burned them outside Jerusalem in the fields of Kidron, and carried their ashes to Bethel. Then he removed the idolatrous priests whom the kings of Judah had ordained to burn incense on the high places in the cities of Judah and in the places all around Jerusalem, and those who burned incense to Baal, to the sun, to the moon, to the constellations, and to all the host of heaven. And he brought out the wooden image from the house of the Lord, to the Brook Kidron outside Jerusalem, burned it at the Brook Kidron and ground it to ashes, and threw its ashes on the graves of the common people...

As Josiah turned, he saw the tombs that were there on the mountain. And he sent and took the bones out of the tombs and burned them on the altar, and defiled it according to the word of the Lord which the man of God proclaimed, who proclaimed these words. Then he said, "What gravestone is this that I see?" So the men of the city told him, "It is the tomb of the man of God who came from Judah and proclaimed these things which you have done against the altar of Bethel." And he said, "Let him alone; let no one move his bones." So they let his bones alone, with the bones of the prophet who came from Samaria.

Now Josiah also took away all the shrines of the high places that were in the cities of Samaria, which the kings of Israel had made to provoke the Lord to anger; and he did to them according to all the deeds he had done in Bethel. He executed all the priests of the high places who were there, on the altars, and burned men's bones on them; and he returned to Jerusalem.

Then the king commanded all the people, saying, "Keep the Passover to the Lord your God, as it is written in this Book of the Covenant." Such a Passover surely had never been held since the days of the judges who judged Israel, nor in all the days of the kings of Israel and the kings of Judah."

What you have just read is an abridged account of the extensive reforms carried out by King Josiah in Judah. His actions, as well as the circumstances that triggered them, are very similar to our situations today. Prior to his ascension to the throne and the subsequent discovery of the Book of the Law, everyone did as he liked, living their lives and conducting the affairs of their nation as if they had total control over their destiny. Expectedly, they continued to fall short of their potentials, while repeatedly exposing themselves to setbacks and defeats.

However, following the sudden discovery of the great Book, where it had been dumped in the temple, Josiah had it read to him and he was horrified to discover that the nation had long derailed from its preordained purpose. He was so overwhelmed with shock and grief that he immediately tore his robes. Thereafter, the king ensured that every citizen of the nation was given a reorientation on the direction the nation was supposed to be going. And collectively, they all decided to retrace their steps and conduct their affairs in accordance with the original guidelines of the Almighty. What followed naturally was a restoration of God's favor and blessings upon the nation.

I believe this template is what every nation of the world needs today to achieve the purpose of God for it. I have provided a breakdown of the reformative steps taken by Josiah and his people to serve as a guide to every individual and nation that has gone through the revelations contained in this book.

1. Acknowledgement of the supremacy of God as the overall designer, ruler and decider of the fate of every nation.

2. Revisiting the blueprint of God for the nation, by paying close attention to the aspirations of the founding fathers, as contained in the national symbols, documents and monuments.

3. Sincere acknowledgement of areas of deviation from God's will and purpose for the nation.

4. Individual and collective rededication of hearts and lives to God Almighty.

5. Individual and collective resolve to adhere strictly to the calling of God upon the nation, as contained in the vision and values established by the founding fathers.

6. Conscientious commitment to dealing decisively with structures, customs and practices that are at variance with the divine calling and foundational values of the nation.

7. Uncompromising resolve to punish evildoers, without sentiment or partiality – as Josiah did to all who had sold themselves to the worship of strange gods.

8. Gracious rewards and commendation for those who have

sacrificed or still sacrificing themselves for the promotion, preservation and propagation of noble values – as it was done to the dead prophet whose grave and remains were spared from destruction.

9. Restoration of all the forgotten, abandoned and relegated foundational values of the nation.

10. Elevating the foundational values of the nation and the ideals of the founding fathers as the guiding light in all matters relating to the affairs of the nation.

Now, it is pertinent that I address this before concluding this book. I have heard some people say that there are nations of the world today that seem not to give a thought to God and yet they seem to be so prosperous and peaceful. Actually, I noted it in the introduction of this book that this has been one area of confusion for many who have a misconception of what greatness is.

Let me explain it here and now that while prosperity and stability could form a part of greatness, they can never be the primary yardstick for measuring true greatness. Jesus proved this when He told the Laodicean church: **"Because you say, "I am rich, have become wealthy, and have need of nothing'—and do not know that you are wretched, miserable, poor, blind, and naked— I counsel you to buy from Me gold refined in the fire, that you may be rich; and white garments, that you may be clothed, that the shame of your nakedness may not be revealed; and anoint your eyes with eye salve, that you may see"** (Revelation 3:17-18).

Let no nation be deceived by the transient facade of prosperity or stability; God's declaration can never be changed: **"The wicked shall be turned into hell, And all the nations that forget God."** (Psalm 9:17). It doesn't matter how long this takes, it will surely happen. If you look at history, you will discover that there have been nations and empires that seemed to enjoy long periods of peace and prosperity despite being godless; yet, when their period of grace was over, it took no time for God to expose them to destruction and devastation.

Think of the previous occupants of the fertile and flourishing land of Canaan, before they were dislodged by the Israelites. Think of Sodom and Gomorrah. Consider the ancient Babylonian, Medo-Persian, Roman and Grecian empires. Think of how long the city Nineveh reveled in godlessness until a warning message of imminent destruction was sent to them.

Even in our contemporary times, we have seen countries that initially seemed invincible and impregnable – but when their time came, they simply crumpled like a pack of cards. When the recent Arab Spring was triggered, most of the nations and leaders affected were those that were previously considered insulated and untouchable but all of a sudden, things fell apart and the centers could no longer hold.

Let this truth forever resonate in every heart and clime: God has and will always be actively involved in the affairs of all nations of the earth. Therefore, to use the words of George Washington, "It is the duty of all nations to acknowledge the providence of Almighty God, to obey His will, to be grateful for His benefits, and humbly to implore His protection and favor."

For the Love of God and Nation.
Dr. Sunday Adelaja.

REFERENCES

PART ONE
NATIONS AS MASTERPIECES OF DESTINY

CHAPTER ONE: NATIONS ARE NOT BY ACCIDENT

1. "Nationalism". https://en.wikipedia.org/wiki/Nationalism
2. Nationalism Studies (2010). "The Formation of Nations". https://nationalismstudies.wordpress.com/2010/03/19/the-formation-of-nations/
3. Rasmussen, P.R. (2001). "Nations" or "States"?: An Attempt at Definition". https://www.globalpolicy.org/nations/nation/2001/0720definition.htm
4. Palaniyapan (2013). "Why Singapore isn't an accidental nation". http://singaporematters.blogspot.com.ng/2013/05/need-to-relook-not-overlook.html

CHAPTER TWO: GOD PREORDAINS NATIONAL PURPOSE

1. Munroe, M. (2002). Understanding the Purpose and Power of Men. Whitaker House.
2. Murray, D. (2015). The Happy Christian: Ten Ways to be a Joyful Believer in a Gloomy World. Nelson Publishers.
3. McNeely, D. (2010). The Decline and Fall of Nations: A Prophetic Perspective". https://www.ucg.org/world.../the-decline-and-fall-of-nations-a-prophetic-perspective

CHAPTER THREE: UNLOCKING GOD'S MASTER PLAN
FOR EVERY NATION

1. Badejo, F.A. (2014). "What value our national symbols?"
   http://smn-news.com/st-maarten-st-martin-news/15872-
   what-value-our-national-symbols.html
2. Elgenius, G. (2005). Expressions of nationhood: national
   symbols and ceremonies in contemporary Europe. PhD
   thesis, The London School of Economics and Political
   Science (LSE).
3. Munroe, M. (2002). Understanding the Purpose and Power
   of Men. Whitaker House.

PART TWO
UNRAVELLING THE CALLINGS OF SPECIFIC NATIONS

CHAPTER FOUR: UNITED STATES OF AMERICA: THE
NATION IN A RENDEZVOUS WITH DESTINY

1. www.forbes.com/sites/.../why-the-u-s-remains-the-
   worlds-unchallenged-superpower/
2. http://www.salon.com/2014/09/18/why_america_will_
   never_win_the_war_on_terror_partner/
3. www.dailymail.co.uk/news/article-400277/Britain-World-
   War-II.html
4. http://www.historydiscussion.net/world-history/how-usa-
   became-the-only-super-power-of-the-world/850
5. https://en.wikipedia.org/wiki/Puritan_migration_to_
   New_England_(1620–40)
6. Kennedy, David and Bailey, Thomas (2001). The American
   Spirit: United States History as Seen by Contemporaries,
   Volume 1. Wadsworth.
7. www.greatseal.com/

CHAPTER FIVE: NIGERIA: THE BLESSED GIANT WITH A THINKING PROBLEM

1. https://www.foreignaffairs.com/articles/nigeria/2010-09-09/nigeria-brink
2. https://thenigerianoracle.wordpress.com/2012/11/08/will-nigeria-break-up-in-2015/#more-4891
3. https://www.theguardian.com/global/2011/jan/04/nigerians-top-optimism-poll
4. Ubaku KC, Emeh CA, Anyikwa CN (2014) Impact of Nationalist movement on the actualization of Nigerian Independence, 1914–1960. International Journal of History and Philosophical Research 2(1): 54–67
5. allafrica.com/stories/201309280265.html
6. http://www.opinionnigeria.com/revisiting-nigerias-foundation-between-what-her-founding-fathers-saw-and-what-nigeria-is-today/#sthash.VE19ewfx.dpbs

CHAPTER SIX: FRANCE: THE SPECTACULAR THINKER WITH A PECULIAR STINKER

1. Hazareesingh, Sudhir (2015). How the French Think: An Affectionate Portrait of an Intellectual People. Basic Books.
2. http://www.pressreader.com/uk/the-guardian-weekly/20150710/281891591942684/TextView
3. Fenby, J. (2015). The History of Modern France: From the Revolution to the Present Day. Simon & Schuster.
4. https://www.marxists.org/archive/jaures/1901/history/causes-revolution.htm
5. www.bbc.com/news/magazine-34843770
6. www.gouvernement.fr/en/marianne-and-the-motto-of-the-republic
7. glennobrien.com/the-mistress-frances-secret-weapon/

8. www.usatoday.com/story/news/world/2014/01/18/france-hollande.../4587251/
9. http://www.telegraph.co.uk/women/sex/11751923/In-France-when-it-comes-to-cheating-everyone-must-remain-discreet.html

CHAPTER SEVEN: GERMANY: THE PACESETTER THROUGH PEACEMAKING

1. kwhs.wharton.upenn.edu/2015/08/germany-drives-the-eurozone/
2. http://www.dw.com/en/why-germans-are-good-at-saving/av-18203387
3. www.bbc.com/news/business-18868704
4. http://business.time.com/2010/09/27/why-you-should-behave-less-like-an-american-and-more-like-a-german/
5. https://en.wikipedia.org/wiki/Reconstruction_of_Germany
6. https://en.wikipedia.org/wiki/Economic_history_of_Germany
7. http://www.econlib.org/library/Enc/GermanEconomicMiracle.html

CHAPTER EIGHT: UNITED KINGDOM: THE PRESERVER OF ANCIENT VALUES

1. www.bbc.com/news/uk-18237280
2. https://www.theatlantic.com/international/archive/2012/02/its-the-queens-60th-anniversary-why-is-britain-still-a-monarchy/252608/
3. Bagehot, Walter (2017). The English Constitution. Jazzybee Verlag.
4. www.telegraph.co.uk › News › UK News › The Royal Family

5. http://royalcentral.co.uk/blogs/insight/top-10-bizarre-traditions-of-the-british-monarchy-24065
6. https://www.theguardian.com/uk/2000/dec/06/monarchy.features11
7. https://www.quora.com/Why-has-the-UK-retained-the-monarchy?page_id=4&redirected_qid=419407
8. http://thejupital.com/popularity-of-the-british-monarchy-leads-queen-elizabeth-to-celebrate-60th-coronation/

PART THREE

ENGRAVING NATIONAL VALUES IN THE CONSCIOUSNESS OF A NATION

CHAPTER NINE: CONNECTION BETWEEN NATIONAL VALUES AND NATIONAL PROGRESS

1. http://thenationonlineng.net/on-national-values/
2. http://www.vanguardngr.com/2011/07/ministerial-nominees-senators-have-limitations-senator-abaribe/
3. https://www.spectator.co.uk/2015/06/2067-the-end-of-british-christianity/#
4. https://www.foreignaffairs.com/articles/western-europe/failure-multiculturalism
5. http://www.independent.co.uk/news/uk/politics/david-cameron-extremism-speech-read-the-transcript-in-full-10401948.html
6. http://www.dw.com/en/german-labor-minister-threatens-non-integrating-refugees-with-welfare-cuts/a-19015000
7. http://dailycaller.com/2016/09/20/sarkozy-to-migrants-if-you-want-to-become-french-you-speak-french/
8. http://www.vanguardngr.com/2017/02/buharis-fight-corruption-not-political-development-lawmaker/
9. http://www.vanguardngr.com/2016/09/noa-launches-

change-begins-programme-dg/
10. http://www.vanguardngr.com/2016/09/buharis-change-begins-with-me-campaign-last-hope-for-nigeria/
11. www.bbc.com/news/business-31369185

CHAPTER TEN: NATIONAL VALUES AND THE EDUCATIONAL SYSTEM

1. Yochelson, Samuel and Samenow, Stanton. (1993). The Criminal Personality. Jason Aronson Inc.
2. http://www.seenmagazine.us/Articles/Article-Detail/ArticleId/4140/EDUCATING-THE-HEAD-HEART-AND-HAND-FOR-THE-21ST-CENTURY
3. http://www.scseec.edu.au/archive/Publications/Publications-archive/The-Adelaide-Declaration.aspx
4. https://guardian.ng/features/history-teaching-in-schools-as-tool-for-national-development/
5. http://nigeriainfo.fm/lagos/local/item/4824-tinubu-advocates-return-of-history-to-school-curriculum?jsn_mobilize_preview=dhxyksaxgb
6. Cheney, Lynne V. (1987). AMERICAN MEMORY: A REPORT ON THE HUMANITIES IN THE NATION'S PUBLIC SCHOOLS. National Endowment for the Humanities.
7. https://nottsteachingbuzz.wordpress.com/2014/05/20/the-benefits-of-roleplay-teaching-history/

CHAPTER ELEVEN: THE MEDIA AS ADVOCATES OF NATIONAL VALUES

1. https://history.hanover.edu/courses/excerpts/165acton.html

CHAPTER TWELVE: RELIGIOUS ORGANIZATIONS AS POWERFUL FORCES FOR INCULCATION OF NATIONAL VALUES AND IDEALS

1. https://berkleycenter.georgetown.edu/posts/holy-healers-and-the-polio-campaign
2. thenationonlineng.net/blame-religious-leaders-corruption-nigeria

CHAPTER THIRTEEN: PRESSURE GROUPS AND CIVIL SOCIETIES AS WATCHDOGS FOR THE VALUES AND IDEALS OF A NATION

1. http://www.vanguardngr.com/2016/07/youths-key-winning-anti-corruption-war-pr-expert/
2. https://www.pmnewsnigeria.com/2012/.../time-to-review-penalty-for-drug-trafficking/

CHAPTER FOURTEEN: THE FAMILY AS AN ENGRAVER AND PROMOTER OF NATIONAL VALUES

1. https://www2.ed.gov/parents/academic/help/citizen/citizen.pdf

SUNDAY ADELAJA'S
BIOGRAPHY

Pastor Sunday Adelaja is the Founder and Senior Pastor of The Embassy of the Blessed Kingdom of God for All Nations Church in Kyiv, Ukraine.

Sunday Adelaja is a Nigerian-born Leader, Thinker, Philosopher, Transformation Strategist, Pastor, Author and Innovator who lives in Kiev, Ukraine.

At 19, he won a scholarship to study in the former Soviet Union. He completed his master's program in Belorussia State University with distinction in journalism.

At 33, he had built the largest evangelical church in Europe — The Embassy of the Blessed Kingdom of God for All Nations.

Sunday Adelaja is one of the few individuals in our world who has been privileged to speak in the United Nations, Israeli Parliament, Japanese Parliament and the United States Senate.

The movement he pioneered has been instrumental in reshaping lives of people in the Ukraine, Russia and about 50 other nations where he has his branches.

His congregation, which consists of ninety-nine percent white Europeans, is a cross-cultural model of the church for the 21st century.

His life mission is to advance the Kingdom of God on earth by

raising a generation of history makers who will live for a cause larger, bigger and greater than themselves. Those who will live like Jesus and transform every sphere of the society in every nation as a model of the Kingdom of God on earth.

His economic empowerment program has succeeded in raising over 200 millionaires in the short period of three years.

Sunday Adelaja is the author of over 300 books, many of which are translated into several languages including Russian, English, French, Chinese, German, etc.

His work has been widely reported by world media outlets such as The Washington Post, The Wall Street Journal, New York Times, Forbes, Associated Press, Reuters, CNN, BBC, German, Dutch and French national television stations.

Pastor Sunday is happily married to his "Princess" Bose Dere-Adelaja. They are blessed with three children: Perez, Zoe and Pearl.

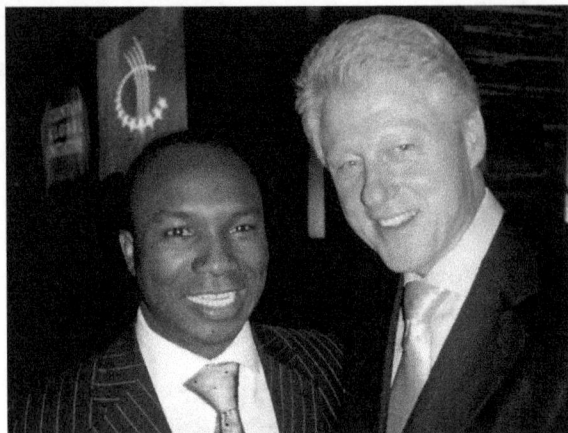

Bill Clinton —
42Nd President Of The
United States (1993–2001),
Former Arcansas State
Governor

Ariel "Arik" Sharon —
Israeli Politician, Israeli
Prime Minister (2001–2006)

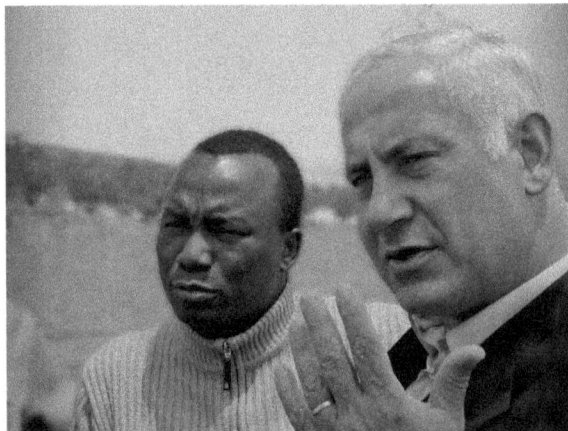

Benjamin Netanyahu —
Statesman Of Israel. Israeli
Prime Minister (1996–1999),
Acting Prime Minister
(From 2009)

Jean ChrEtien —
Canadian Politician,
20Th Prime Minister Of
Canada, Minister Of Justice
Of Canada, Head Of Liberan
Party Of Canada

Rudolph Giuliani —
American Political Actor,
Mayor Of New York Served
From 1994 To 2001. Actor
Of Republican Party

Colin Powell —
Is An American Statesman
And A Retired Four-Star
General In The Us Army,
65Th United States Secretary
Of State

Peter J. Daniels —
Is A Well-Known And
Respected Australian
Christian International
Business Statesman Of
Substance

Madeleine
Korbel Albright —
An American Politician And
Diplomat, 64Th United States
Secretary Of State

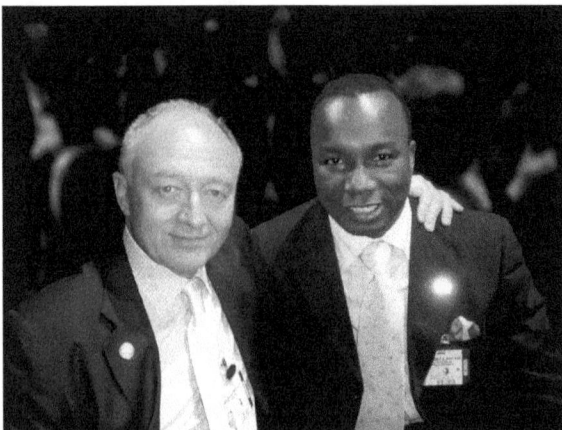

Kenneth Robert
Livingstone —
An English Politician,
1St Mayor Of London
(4 May 2000 – 4 May
2008), Labour Party
Representative

Sir Richard Charles Nicholas
Branson —
English Business
Magnate, Investor And
Philanthropist. He Founded
The *Virgin Group*,
Which Controls More Than
400 Companies

Mel Gibson —
American Actor
And Filmmaker

Chuck Norris —
American Martial Artist,
Actor, Film Producer And
Screenwriter

Christopher Tucker —
American Actor
And Comedian

Bernice Albertine King —
American Minister Best
Known As The Youngest
Child Of Civil Rights Leaders
Martin Luther King Jr. And
Coretta Scott King Andrew

Andrew Young — American
Politician, Diplomat, And
Activist, 14[Th] United States
Ambassador To The United
Nations, 55[Th] Mayor Of
Atlanta

General Wesley
Kanne Clark —
4-Star General And Nato
Supreme Allied Commander

Dr. Sunday Adelaja's family:
Perez, Pearl, Zoe and Pastor Bose Adelaja

FOLLOW
SUNDAY ADELAJA
ON SOCIAL MEDIA

Subscribe And Read Pastor Sunday's Blog:

www.sundayadelajablog.com

Follow these links and listen to over 200

of Pastor Sunday`s Messages free of charge:

http://sundayadelajablog.com/content/

Follow Pastor Sunday on Twitter:

www.twitter.com/official_pastor

Join Pastor Sunday's Facebook page to stay in touch:

www.facebook.com/pastor.

sunday.adelaja

Visit our websites for more

information about Pastor

Sunday's ministry:

http://www.godembassy.com

http://www.pastorsunday.com

http://sundayadelaja.de

CONTACT

FOR DISTRIBUTION OR TO ORDER
BULK COPIES OF THIS BOOK,
PLEASE CONTACT US:

USA
CORNERSTONE PUBLISHING
info@thecornerstonepublishers.com
+1 (516) 547-4999
www.thecornerstonepublishers.com

AFRICA
CHIOMA NWIGWE (NIGERIA)
dsabooksplanet@gmail.com
+2347065228537, +2348122219291

LONDON, UK
ADEKUNLE BANJOKO
banjokoadekunle@gmail.com
+447411937793

KIEV, UKRAINE
pa@godembassy.org
Mobile: +380674401958

BEST SELLING BOOKS BY DR. SUNDAY ADELAJA
AVAILABLE ON AMAZON.COM AND OKADABOOKS.COM

MONEY WON'T make you Rich
GOD'S PRINCIPLES FOR TRUE WEALTH, PROSPERITY AND SUCCESS
SUNDAY ADELAJA

NIGERIA AND THE LEADERSHIP QUESTION
"IF NIGERIA DOES NOT SUCCEED, WHO ELSE CAN SUCCEED?"
— PETER EIGEN, TRANSPARENCY INTERNATIONAL (GERMANY)
PROFFERING SOLUTIONS TO NIGERIA'S LEADERSHIP PROBLEM
SUNDAY ADELAJA
BEST SELLING AUTHOR OF CHURCHSHIFT

MYLES MUNROE
... FINDING ANSWERS TO WHY GOOD PEOPLE DIE TRAGIC AND EARLY DEATHS
SUNDAY ADELAJA

THE KINGDOM DRIVEN LIFE
Thy Kingdom Come, Thy will be Done on Earth . . .
SUNDAY ADELAJA
BEST SELLING AUTHOR OF CHURCHSHIFT

CHURCH SHIFT
SUNDAY ADELAJA

WHO AM I?
WHY AM I HERE?
SUNDAY ADELAJA
BEST SELLING AUTHOR OF CHURCHSHIFT

ONLY GOD can save NIGERIA: What a Myth!
SUNDAY ADELAJA
The Author of Nigeria and the Leadership Question

STOP WORKING FOR UNCLE SAM
SUNDAY ADELAJA

The MOUNTAIN of IGNORANCE
The Greatest Problem of Man is Not Sin or Satan, It is Ignorance
SUNDAY ADELAJA

OLORUNWA
ЗОЛОТОЙ КЛЮЧ К БОГАТОЙ ЖИЗНИ

INSULTED by UNGODLINESS
RAISING A GENERATION OF THE PROVOKED IN EVERY NATION
SUNDAY ADELAJA
BEST SELLING AUTHOR OF CHURCHSHIFT

HOW TO REGAIN YOUR LOST YEARS
SUNDAY ADELAJA

HOW TO BUILD A SECURED FINANCIAL FUTURE
IT DOES NOT MATTER HOW MUCH YOU MAKE, IF YOU ARE IGNORANT OF THE LAWS OF MONEY YOU WILL NEVER BE RICH
SUNDAY ADELAJA

CREATE YOUR OWN NET WORTH
YOUR MONEY IS TEMPORARY, YOUR NET WORTH IS ETERNAL
SUNDAY ADELAJA
THE AUTHOR OF MONEY WON'T MAKE YOU RICH

RAISING THE NEXT GENERATION OF STEVE JOBS AND BILL GATES
HOW TO CONVERT YOUR INNER ENERGY INTO TANGIBLE PRODUCTS
SUNDAY ADELAJA

POVERTY MINDSET VS ABUNDANCE MINDSET
REAL POVERTY IS NOT IN THE SIZE OF YOUR POCKET BUT IN THE SIZE OF YOUR MIND
SUNDAY ADELAJA

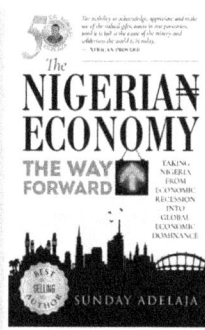

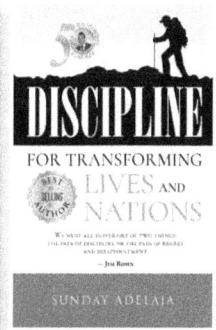

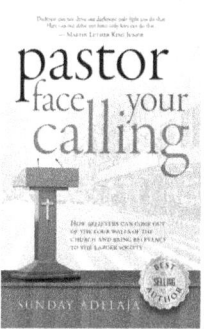

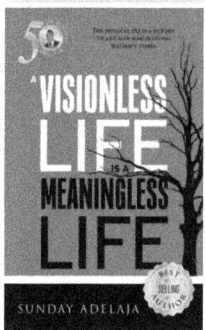

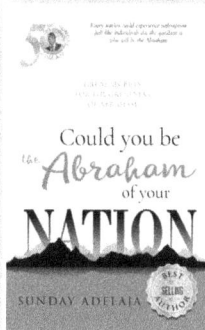

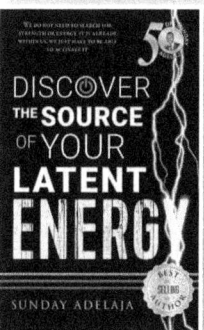

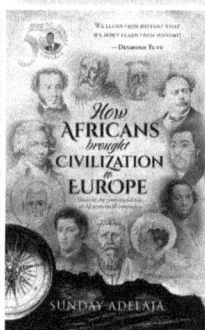

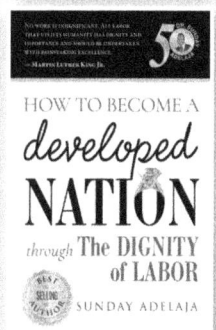

BEST SELLING BOOKS BY DR. SUNDAY ADELAJA
AVAILABLE ON AMAZON.COM AND OKADABOOKS.COM

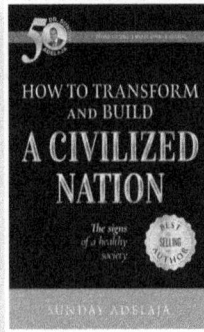

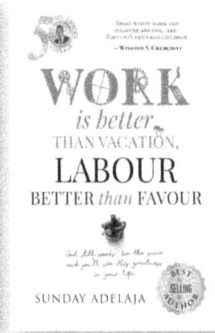

Best Selling Books by Dr. Sunday Adelaja
Available on Amazon.com and Okadabooks.com

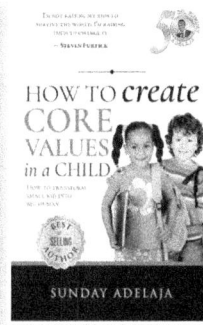

DON'T EAT TOMORROW'S FOOD TODAY
How to escape financial slavery
SUNDAY ADELAJA

WHY LOSING YOUR JOB is the best thing THAT COULD HAPPEN TO YOU
SUNDAY ADELAJA

I AM A PERSON, am I a PERSONALITY
SUNDAY ADELAJA

HOW TO create CORE VALUES in a CHILD
SUNDAY ADELAJA

Golden Jubilee Series Books by Dr. Sunday Adelaja

FOR DISTRIBUTION OR TO ORDER BULK COPIES OF THIS BOOKS, PLEASE CONTACT US:

USA | CORNERSTONE PUBLISHING
E-mail: info@thecornerstonepublishers.com, +1 (516) 547-4999
www.thecornerstonepublishers.com

AFRICA | CHIOMA NWIGWE (NIGERIA)
E-mail: dsabooksplanet@gmail.com
+2347065228537, +2348122219291

LONDON, UK | ADEKUNLE BANJOKO
E-mail: banjokoadekunle@gmail.com, +447411937793

KIEV, UKRAINE |
E-mail: pa@godembassy.org, Mobile: +380674401958